CRASHING
COMPUTERS

The Knowledge

CRASHING COMPUTERS

MICHAEL COLEMAN

Illustrated by
Mike Phillips

Hippo

Scholastic Children's Books,
Commonwealth House, 1–19 New Oxford Street,
London WC1A 1NU, UK
a division of Scholastic Ltd
London ~ New York ~ Toronto ~ Sydney ~ Auckland
Mexico City ~ New Delhi ~ Hong Kong

Published in the UK by Scholastic Ltd, 1999

ISBN 0 590 11425 5

Typeset by TW Typesetting, Midsomer Norton
Printed and bound by Nørhaven Paperback, Viborg, Denmark

14 16 18 20 19 17 15 13

The right of Michael Coleman and Mike Phillips to be identified
as the author and illustrator of this work respectively has been
asserted by them in accordance with the Copyright, Designs and
Patents Act, 1988.

Contents

To John Coleman – my computer Whizz-Dad

Introduction

Have your teachers ever called you lazy? If so, they were right (for once)!

Have you ever called your teachers lazy (under your breath, of course)? Then you were right too!

That's because human beings are *all* lazy – and there's plenty of evidence to prove it...

▶ we've invented motor cars, to save us the effort of walking to the shops to buy food

▶ we've invented gas cookers, to save us the effort of making a fire to cook the food we've just bought

▶ we've even invented TV remote controls, to save us the effort of getting up to switch channels while we're eating the food we've just cooked!

Ever since time began we humans have been thinking of things to make life easier for ourselves. Unfortunately, thinking is itself very hard work. So, what quickly became the top dream for us lazy humans? Machines that would do our thinking for us, of course!

Machines such as these have taken a long time to develop, but over the past few years they've made amazing progress – so amazing, that nowadays you can find them everywhere.

You've probably got a few of them at home. There's the sort you play games on, of course, but if you pull the video recorder and the washing machine to pieces you'll find some inside them too.

Have a look round your school as well. You'll almost certainly find a few of the most recent types of these machines dotted about. They're dead easy to spot: they've all got keyboards and screens, and the teachers are scared of them.

Yes, we're talking about the computer! They're everywhere nowadays, doing hundreds and hundreds of our thinking jobs. In this book you'll discover just a selection of the jobs computers are doing for us.

But...

You'll also find out some of the jobs they're not doing, as well! Because, fantastic as they are, there's one way in which the computer is no different to every other human invention. They can stop working!

Cars sometimes break down. Gas cookers sometimes explode. TV remote controls sometimes get trodden on (usually when you're looking for them). And computers can go wrong. Like...

▶ the computer that lost a spacecraft!

▶ the computer that invited a 104 year-old lady to join a nursery school!

▶ the computer that got itself arrested!

So in this book you'll not only find out what computers can do, you'll also read about the sort of things that can happen when they go wrong.

That is, when they become ... "crashing" computers!

Crashing Computer Timeline - Part 1

Ever since humans realized that using their fingers only helped them count up to ten (and taking their socks off didn't help much more) the search was on for a quicker way of doing their maths homework – that is, of "computing". Although bead-counting devices like the abacus had been around since 3000 BC, nothing much happened for another 4,500 years...

1623 With metalworking becoming much more exact, Wilhelm Schickard of Germany builds a "calculator-clock" able to multiply two six-digit numbers together. It was reconstructed in 1960, and it worked.

1642 French inventor Blaise Pascal builds a machine to help his tax collector Dad work out how much tax people owe. It's the first digital calculator. Called a "Pascaline", it adds together columns of numbers. It works well, too, until Dad tries a sum like 99999 + 1 and all the moving parts get stuck as it tries to turn

GIVE ME AN HOUR AND I'LL LET YOU KNOW THE TIME

IT'S SOMETHING THE WORLD NEEDS

A NUTCRACKER?

ADDING THIS LOT UP IS SUM JOB!

the 9's into 0's — which must have taxed Dad's patience a lot!

1673 Another German mathematician, Gottfried Leibniz, builds a mechanical calculator that multiplies, divides, adds and subtracts.

1822 Englishman Charles Babbage designs a machine called a "Difference Engine" to calculate maths tables. This machine never, ever crashes. Why not? Because Babbage doesn't finish making it!

1833 Babbage designs a much more advanced machine. This one is different to every other calculating machine that's been thought of so far. Called an "Analytical Machine", it's designed not just to do maths but to obey a **program** (a set of instructions). This machine never goes wrong either — but not because Babbage doesn't finish it. It's because it's

HAVE YOU BEEN OVER TAXING THIS MACHINE, DAD?

I CALL IT A "DIFFERENCE ENGINE"

THE DIFFERENCE IS THAT IT'S NOT FINISHED!

THIS NEW MACHINE IS FAR BETTER THAN THE DIFFERENCE ENGINE

SO WAS A PEN AND PAPER!

never even started! The Analytical Machine is so complicated nobody knows how to make it!

And yet, in spite of these two failures, Babbage is known today as the "Father of Computing"...

"Barmy" Babbage and the Cool Countess

Charles Babbage (1791–1871) is famous in the world of computers because, even though he failed to put his ideas into practice, many of them were so brainy and ahead of their time that they can still be seen in the design of modern-day computers. During his life, though, many people didn't think Babbage was brainy at all – they thought he was completely barmy!

So, "Brainy" Babbage or "Barmy" Babbage? Weigh up the evidence for yourself!

Brainy: He was made Professor of Mathematics at Cambridge University.

Barmy: He never gave a lecture, but spent all his time inventing things!

Brainy: The Government thought so – for a while at least. Convinced by Babbage's claims that his Difference Engine would perform calculations far more accurately than any machine had ever done before, they gave him £17,000 to help fund his work.

Barmy: Babbage's design was so advanced that before parts of it could be made he had to invent the tools to do the job! Then, when all was finally ready, he had a furious argument with his engineer – who walked out, never to return!

Brainy: Babbage wasn't too concerned, though, because by then (1833) he'd designed his Analytical Engine. This would be a far better machine, one that could perform lots of different calculations by following a program of instructions. What's more, it would be able to **store** (remember) these results and print them out on paper! This is exactly what a modern computer does!

Barmy: Unfortunately, the Government had changed its mind. They now thought Babbage was off his head and refused to give him any more money. One opponent said: "We got nothing for our £17,000 but Babbage's grumblings!"

Brainy: Not all Babbage's inventions went the same way. Trains had not long been invented and he was mad about them. As track began to cross open countryside Babbage was the first to see a possible problem ... so he sat down and invented – the cowcatcher!

Barmy: He was also intrigued by fire. He even went as far as having himself lowered into a volcano so that he could get a closer look at molten lava! On another occasion he had himself baked in an oven at 124°C (265°F) for five minutes, emerging quite happily afterwards "without any discomfort".

Brainy: Babbage loved facts. He couldn't stop collecting them.

Barmy: Unfortunately, many of these facts were completely potty! For instance, he once investigated 464 broken windows and listed how they came to get smashed. Talk about a pane-full exercise!

Brainy: He also worked out that 25 percent of his brain-power was lost because of the noise outside his house caused by street entertainers.

Barmy: That's what his neighbours thought when Babbage campaigned to have entertainers banned. They tormented him by leaving nasty things on his doorstep (like dead cats!) and a brass band once deliberately stood under his window and played for five hours. No wonder Babbage wanted the band banned!

So, do you think Babbage was "brainy" or "barmy"? Although two Swedes, George and Edvard Scheutz of Stockholm, built the first practical mechanical computer based on Babbage's work in 1855, the real proof didn't come until 1991.

Then, to celebrate the 200th anniversary of his birth, the Difference Engine Babbage had designed but never completed was actually made at the Science Museum in London. It had 4,000 parts, was 3.3 m (11 ft) long and 2.1 m (7 ft) high, and weighed three tonnes. What's more, when it was tried out – it worked!

There was now no doubt about it. Babbage may have been slightly barmy but he was mostly brainy!

Crashing fact
After Babbage died his brain was pickled. It was kept until 1908, when a surgeon cut it up to see if it looked like a normal brain. Whether he was looking for signs of intelligence or madness isn't known!

Through all his problems, Charles Babbage could always count on the help of a cool Countess. Her name was Ada, Countess of Lovelace. She became fascinated with the idea of the Analytical Engine after hearing Babbage talk about it at a dinner party.

Maybe they got on so famously because Ada was both brainy and barmy as well. She was certainly barmy enough to believe Babbage when he claimed he could use mathematics to calculate the winners of horse races – she only just avoided losing all her money through following his rotten tips!

She was a very good amateur mathematician, though, and one of the few people who realized how powerful a working Analytical Engine would be...

Ada wrote a plan describing how the analytical engine might perform some mathematical calculations. It's now regarded as the first "computer program."

Crashing fact

A programming language developed by the U.S. Department of Defense in 1979 was named "Ada" in honour of Countess Lovelace.

Crashing Computer Timeline – Part 2

1886 Herman Hollerith of Buffalo, New York builds a tabulating machine which works by means of cards with holes punched in them. His company grows and merges with others until...

1924 It changes its name to International Business Machines – IBM, for short. Thomas Watson is the company's first chairman. One of his first actions is to have posters stuck up everywhere telling his employees what he wants them to do. The posters have one word on them: "THINK" And that's what they do. IBM grows into the biggest computer company in the world.

1939 (to 1942) John V. Atanasoff of the USA designs and builds a calculating machine called ABC*. It's the first

*The Atanasoff Berry Computer. Atanasoff was helped by electronical engineering student Clifford Berry

recognizable electronic digital computer because some electrical components have taken the place of the usual clock-like wheels and levers.

1941 (to 1944): The first all-electric calculating machine is designed and built by Tommy Flowers in England. It's called *Colossus* – but, officially, it doesn't exist! It's being used to crack the codes used by Adolf Hitler's top secret messages during World War II, so it has to be even more top secret.

Crashing fact

Colossus was so top secret it was destroyed after the war and the people who worked with it were forbidden to talk about it. So when a judge decided in 1973 that Atanasoff's ABC was the first working computer, nobody from England was allowed to put him straight!

1943 (to 1945): in the USA, the first general-purpose computer is built at the University of Pennsylvania. It's called ENIAC (Electronic Numerical Integrator and Computer) and can run different programs. Switching from one program to another isn't easy, though: the whole thing has to be re-wired!

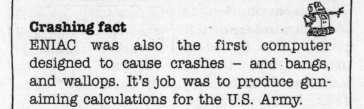

1940 Everything starts going mad ... because MAD (Manchester Automatic Digital) Machine Mk 1 goes into action in 1948! Controlled by switches that have been salvaged from old fighter plane radios, it's the first computer that can obey a stored program and is nicknamed "Baby" – probably short for baby elephant because it's 4.5 m (16 ft) long, 2.5 m (7 ft) high and 0.75 m (2 ft) deep!

1947 The days of the dinosaur-sized computer are already numbered. A device called a transistor is invented. It does the same job as the fat tubes used in computers till now, but is much smaller.

19

The magazine *Popular Mechanics* is so excited it predicts that computers may one day weigh no more than 1½ tonnes!

1952 In the USA, a computer is used to forecast an election result for the first time. It doesn't go wrong but, when it surprisingly predicts that outsider Dwight Eisenhower will win, everybody thinks it has! Frightened of looking silly, the operators reprogram the machine – only to look really silly as the computer's original prediction comes true!

1967 The first computer-controlled cashpoint machine is unveiled at Barclays Bank in Enfield, London. This time the computer is working well; it's Sir Thomas Bland, the chairman of the Bank, who isn't. He simply can't understand what to do. So when the TV cameras

turn up, a hidden bank employee has to push some money out to him by hand!

1969 Now the days of transistorized computers are numbered as the *silicon chip*, or *microchip**, (known as integrated circuits, or IC – the foundation of modern computers) is invented. It's the start of the smaller computer, and a million corny jokes about "chips with everything"!

1975 The first personal computer, the Altair, goes on sale. Forget about the keyboards and screens of today, though. Information was fed into it by clicking switches and results were shown on a set of flickering lights. And all that only happened once you'd put the thing together – it was supplied as a build-it-yourself kit!

1980 Computers crash

---

*Microchips are circuits on tiny bits of silicon, covered in a plastic casing.

into the TV schedules! The BBC broadcasts a series about computers and a "BBC Microcomputer" is marketed to go with it. Expecting to sell only 10,000 the manufacturers, Acorn, end up selling millions – particularly to schools and colleges. (Look around. There may still be one, covered in cobwebs, in a classroom near you!)

Early 1980s Computers crash down chimneys! The top-selling Christmas present for children is a home computer, the Sinclair Spectrum. It's a keyboard and computer combined, plugs into a TV, and plays games. But what really makes it a winner is … the screen displays are in colour, not black and white!

1981 IBM introduces its first *PC* (Personal Computer). From now on, the majority of personal computers in the world follow the same design –

and are said to be "PC-compatible".

1984 The exception is the series of PCs built by the company Apple, in particular the Apple "Macintosh" ("Mac" for short). Instead of expecting slow-typing users to key in commands, Apple Macs are friendlier – they work by having users point at symbols on the computer's screen. Stun your teacher and call it by its proper name – a "graphical interface".

1985 A similar look is given to IBM PC's by a system called "Windows" from the company Microsoft. This company had been formed in 1975 by two college students, Bill Gates and Paul Allen.

1985 onwards

Computers get smaller and faster. But how small, and how fast?

23

How small?

Think of it this way. The 1948 computer "Baby" measured 4.5 m (16 ft) wide by 2.5 m (7 ft) high. In order to have had same amount of memory as a typical PC today, it would have had to be about 90 km (50 miles) wide and nearly four times as high as Mount Everest!

How fast?

The ENIAC computer of 1945 could perform 360 multiplications per second. Better than you or me, perhaps, but today the most powerful computer in the world can do 1 million million calculations per second. If human athletes had improved as much, sprinters able to run 100 m in 10 seconds in 1945 would now be able to race round the planet 7,000 times instead!

Today PCs come in all shapes and sizes. They sit on desks and are carried under arms. (There are so many around, and new ones are produced so quickly, that in the USA an estimated 10 million PCs are dumped every year). As for Bill Gates, the founder of Microsoft, he's still going strong...

The crashing computer whizz-kid

Try this exercise. (Unless you know somebody with even more money than Bill Gates, it will have to be in your imagination.)

- ▶ Every single second of the day, put £1 into your piggy bank.
- ▶ Keep going for a week. You'll now have £604,800.
- ▶ Keep going. By day 12, you'll be a

millionaire!

► Keep going. During the 4th month you'll pass £10 million

► Keep going. After just over 3 years you'll be worth £100 million

Well done! But you're still not as rich as Bill Gates. To catch him up, you'll have to...

► Keep putting £1 into your piggy bank every second of every day for another 300 years!

That's how rich Bill Gates is. And he's getting richer every day. It's estimated that in 1997 his fortune increased by about £30 million – per day!

So how could you do the same? Here are your ten top tips on how to become a crashing computer whizz-kid.

1 Forget comics and read business magazines instead. When Bill Gates was ten his favourite reading was a magazine called "Fortune".

2 Learn all you can about how businesses make money. Gates' favourite game at his boarding school was writing off for details of successful companies.

3 Sweet-talk your Mum! Gates' school had a telephone connection to a computer which had to be paid for by the students who used it. They got

their Mums to raise money for them by holding jumble sales!

4 Play computer games. One of the ways Gates learned about computers was by writing a program to play noughts-and-crosses.

5 Think of other ways to raise money for computer time. When the jumble sale money ran out, Gates persuaded computer companies to pay him for testing their programs. Then, when he found a mistake, he got them to pay him to fix it.

6 Don't bother about sleep. Gates would work on the computer all night, and have a snooze during classes the next day.

7 When you're 18 and go off to college, don't let classes get in the way of your computer work there either. Gates went to Harvard. In his first year he didn't go to a single class in Economics, one of his subjects, but just worked through the books the week before the exam. He scored an A.

8 Give up college altogether. Gates never finished his Harvard course. When he saw the potential of the personal computer, he left to form Microsoft.

9 Play cards. Much of the money Gates used to set up Microsoft had been won playing poker against other students.

10 Be a business genius. Gates went on to earn his fortune by realizing that it's better to sell millions of inexpensive programs than a

just a few expensive ones. It's been estimated that every day, 90% of the world's personal computers run Microsoft programs – and, since 50 million PCs are sold every year worldwide, that's a lot of programs!

Crashing fact

Bill Gates isn't the only person to have made a lot of money from computers. Charles Babbage did too. Unfortunately it wasn't when he needed it, but after he'd been dead for 120 years. In 1995 his first unfinished Difference Engine was sold for £176,750!

Fast, But Stupid: A Beginners Guide to Computers

How do computers work? What can they do – and what can't they do? A good way to find out is to pretend to be one for a while. You could do it first thing tomorrow morning...

1 **Don't wake up until somebody calls you.** Computers need electricity or batteries, so they can't do a thing until somebody plugs them in or turns them on.

2 **Learn everything you ever learnt all over again.** When they're turned off, computers lose the information in their memory; they have to read it all in again, either from disks or CDs. Until this has happened, they're a waste of space.

3 **Now do what you're told to do, even if it's stupid.** Computers obey instructions they've been given by humans. Most of these instructions will be in the form of computer programs, such as a word processor. Others are given when the program is used – like, "check my spelling", or "rub out the essay I've been typing all night". Computers obey every instruction they're given, whether or not it's sensible. You didn't want to rub out your essay? Tough!

4 **Do everything fantastically quickly**. A few billion long multiplications while you're brushing your teeth should give you the idea.

5 **Don't get tired.** No breaks allowed. Computers work flat out and non-stop.

6 **Don't get bored.** Computers are happy to do the

same thing day after day without m

7 Save and remember everything
without the slightest mistake – u
turned off, anyway. Then you can
lot until you're switched on again

That's a bit what it's like to be a computer. But what actually goes on under a computer's cover? Can anybody understand how they work, or do you need to have the intelligence of a top secret agent...?

"Boldfinger" – or learning the Binary Code

The laboratory door thumped open. A hat whizzed across the room and landed neatly on a peg. In stepped a cool dude wearing a dinner jacket and a bow tie.

"The name's Bond," he announced. "Premium Bond. Top secret agent."

A grey-haired professor looked up from his bench and sighed. "Stop acting the fool, 003½."

Premium frowned. Hearing his number reminded him of a question that had been taxing him for a long time. "How come I'm agent 003½ and the other Bond is 007?"

"Because he's a wit and you're a half-wit. For a start he can remember big numbers."

"I can remember big numbers."

"How big?" asked the professor.

Premium began counting on his fingers. "Er ... up to ten."

"Not much good when we send you out to destroy the spy ring living at number 216 Enemy Avenue, is it? Why do you use your fingers anyway?"

"Because they're really handy!" grinned Premium.

"And because you've got a rotten memory," snapped the professor. "Which is why I'm going to explain binary code to you."

"Binary? What's that? Anything to do with bicycles?"

The professor nodded. "In a way."

And awful thought struck Premium. "You're not taking away my lovely fast car? I can't bomb around the countryside shaking off enemy agents on a bike! What will I do with my machine guns, strap 'em to the crossbar?"

"No, no. Binary code is what computers use. And the way it's connected to a bicycle is that they both use the number 2."

"Right!" sighed Premium in relief. "Bicycles use two wheels and binary code uses two ... er – two what?"

The professor didn't answer at once. "Hands up!" he snapped.

Premium reached for the sky. "Don't shoot! I'll tell you everything you want to know!"

"This isn't a stick-up, Bond. Now, look at your fingers. What are they doing?"

Premium looked up at his hands. "They're sticking up, of course! And you said this wasn't a stick-up!"

"Now make a fist. As if you're going to punch me."

"Ah, now we're getting somewhere," said Premium, folding his fingers down.

The professor ducked behind his bench. "Now think," he shouted. "First your fingers were up. Then they were down. Two positions. That is what a binary code is all about."

Premium thought carefully about this. "But ... that means I'll only be able to use my hands to count up to two!"

"No, you won't," said the professor, creeping out again. "Because each of your fingers can be either up or down."

"Don't forget my thumbs," corrected Premium. "Everybody says I'm all fingers and thumbs."

"Making ten binary digits in all. Or, in computer jargon, ten bits you can use for counting. A bit is short for binary digit. What you might call – shorthand!" the professor chuckled.

"So how do computers use these bits for counting, then?"

"Simple. When each bit is OFF – that is, when your finger or thumb is down – it stands for nothing. When it's on, it stands for a number."

"What number?" asked Premium.

The professor pulled out a pen and wrote on each of Premium's finger nails.

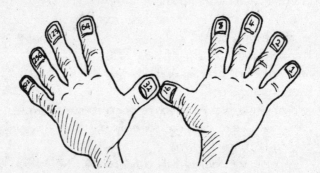

"Notice anything?" he asked.

"I'd better become left-handed," Premium nodded. "That one's worth a lot more than my right!"

"That's because each bit is worth twice the bit on its right. So, come on. If we said you were to go and spy on the occupant of hotel room No. 16, would you be able to remember that number now?"

The agent thought for a bit then just stuck his right thumb up.

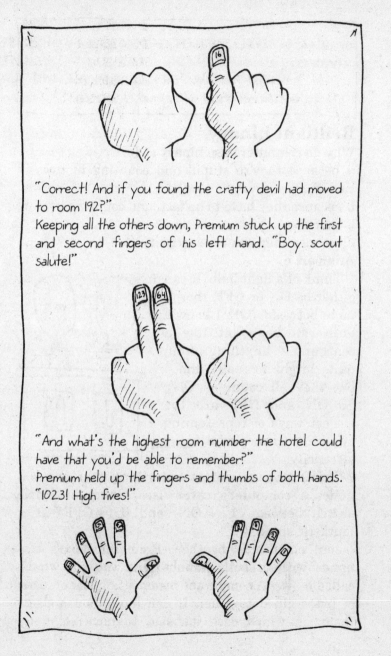

"Correct! And if you found the crafty devil had moved to room 192?"

Keeping all the others down, Premium stuck up the first and second fingers of his left hand. "Boy. scout salute!"

"And what's the highest room number the hotel could have that you'd be able to remember?"

Premium held up the fingers and thumbs of both hands. "1023! High fives!"

"512+256+128+64+32+16+8+4+2+1" agreed the professor. "Excellent!"

"Yeah!" shouted Premium. "Eat your heart out, 007! This is one secret agent who's really hand-sum!"

Brilliant binary

Why do computers use binary code?

a because they're stupid and counting in twos is easiest

b because they have to be fast, and counting in twos is quickest

c because they run on electricity

Answer: c

Think of a light bulb. It can either be ON or OFF, there's no in between. (OK, I know a bulb can be a bit like a teacher – anything from quite bright to really dim – but they all count as ON). So ON and OFF are the easiest ways of representing anything when you're using electricity.

That's why absolutely everything that goes on under a computer's cover uses binary bits that switch between 1 (=ON) and 0 (=OFF) at a fantastic speed.

Join eight bits together (Premium Bond's two hands without both thumbs) and you get what's called a *byte*. A computer's *memory* is made of loads of bytes glued together. It can have thousands of them (in which case it's said to have so many

34

kilobytes, or *Kb*), millions of them (*megabytes*, or *Mb*) or thousands of millions of bytes (*gigabytes*, or *Gb*).

What's more, bytes are like building blocks. You can stick them together, and this is how computers manage to work not just with numbers, but with different types of information...

Easy as ABC

Computers hold letters and symbols (like + £ $!) in binary. The difference is that these strings of 1's and 0's aren't treated numbers but as patterns of 1's and 0's. For instance:

$$0\ 0\ 1\ 0\ 0\ 0\ 0\ 1$$

is the pattern for the letter "A".

Letter "B" is the next pattern in sequence (00100010) and so on. A space has a code, too (00100000). So any word or sentence is stored as a chunk of bytes, with every byte holding a single character. For instance, the message:

CALL A CAB

(00100011)(00100001)(00101100)(00101100)
    C   A   L   L

(00100000)(00100001)(00100000)
 SPACE   A   SPACE

(00100011)(00100001)(00100010)
   C   A   B

Collections of colours

Colours are stored in a similar way to letters, but in this case with each pattern of bits standing for a different colour. So a single byte, which is able to take on any one of 256 different patterns (00000000 though to 11111111) could be used represent 256 different colours.

Question: How could you use just 2 bits to represent the three colours red, green and blue *and* say whether they're on or off?

Answer: 00 = off; 01 = red; 10 = green; 11 = blue

Perfect pictures

You want to display a picture of yourself? No problem. But just remember – you may think you look handsome/gorgeous, but as far as the computer is concerned you'll just be a big blob of binary.

Pictures are stored by dividing them up into tiny squares called "pixels" (short for picture element). Then, for each pixel, one or more bytes is used to store not only the colour but also other information such as brightness. The more pixels used, the better the picture (if you can't see why, imagine your picture divided into just eight pixels, each of which had to be a single colour!). But the more pixels you use, the more memory you'll need.

Serious sounds

The same goes for sounds. Symphony or squawk, the sounds are divided up into their individual notes and stored in binary, with bit patterns representing such things as the note itself – and the volume it's to be played at!

Interesting instructions

Numbers, letters, pictures and sounds are the information, or *data*, the computer program works on. But the program itself has to be stored in the computer's memory too. How? As bytes of binary, of course!

Every type of instruction ("add", "subtract", "multiply" and so on) will have its own binary code. But that's not enough. An "add" instruction, say, needs two numbers to add together. So more bytes will be used to say whereabouts in the memory these numbers are to be found – and where the answer is to be put.

Crashing calculations

Binary may be brilliant, but even computers don't always come up with the right answers. A pocket calculator is a simple computer. Try this little test on it.

▶ Key in the number 100
▶ Divide by 3
▶ Multiply by 3

Now everybody knows that if you divide A by B, then multiply the answer by B, you should get back to A again. The trouble is, computers don't! They're thickos, remember. So the chances are that the

answer you've got isn't 100, as it should be, but
something like 99.9999999

This is why computers sometimes get their sums
wrong. The true answer to a division like 100/3 is a
number which goes on for ever –

$$33.33333333...$$

As only so much of the number can be stored, the
tiddly bits at the end have to be thrown away. This
means that when a second calculation is performed
the tiddly bits aren't there to be used – and the
answer isn't exact as it should be.

$$33.33333333*3 = 99.99999999$$

These tiddly bits are known as "rounding errors"
and they're usually so small it doesn't matter. (Some
maths wizards spend all their time proving that
rounding errors don't matter – it sends them round
the bend!) Sometimes, though, even the tiddliest of
tiddly bits can grow into something that does
matter...

▶ When the St Alban's Council computer worked
out how many people should be paying Council
Tax it didn't come up with a whole number of
people, but with an answer 97384.7! Either the
0.7 of a person was a rounding error – or it was
somebody who wasn't all there!

▶ A more serious rounding error showed up in a
computer-controlled anti-missile system. It was

being used during the Gulf War to detect missiles aimed at Saudi Arabia – but, on 25th February 1991, the system failed and a missile got through. Why? Because the clock used by the computer was about 0.25 of a second out. The designers had ignored rounding errors that made it to lose 1 millionth of a second every second because they'd expected the system to be turned off and the clock reset every day. Nobody had mentioned this to the soldiers, though. The error had grown because they'd had the system working non-stop for nearly 5 days!

Beware! Hardware and software

The basic steps every computer follows aren't terribly new. They've been known since the days of Og the Caveman...

Input, processing and output are the three basic actions of any computer system. For instance, a computer running a word processing program will receive inputs (like the words and sentences of one of your brilliant essays), process them (by chucking yer spilling, I mean checking your spelling) and then output the results (an essay with no spelling mistakes).

The parts of the computer system you can see are known as the *hardware* of the system. Og the Caveman's hardware amounted to:

▶ an *input device* – his mouth
▶ a *processor* – his stomach (OK, you'd have to open him up to see that, but it's the same with a computer. It's "insides" do the processing)
▶ an *output device* – his ... well, there's no need to get to the bottom of that particular subject!

Here are the usual hardware parts of any computer system – and some crashing facts to go with them!

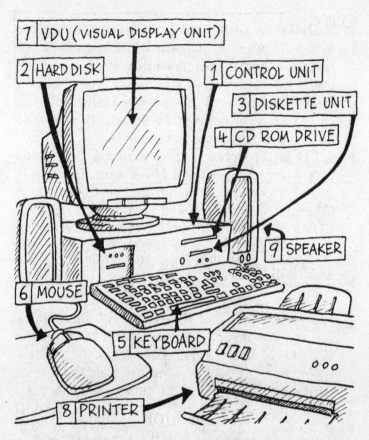

7 VDU (VISUAL DISPLAY UNIT)
2 HARD DISK
1 CONTROL UNIT
3 DISKETTE UNIT
4 CD ROM DRIVE
9 SPEAKER
6 MOUSE
5 KEYBOARD
8 PRINTER

▶ **1 Control unit** – the computer's "body". Inside you'll find the processing and memory chips and circuits that do all the work.

▶ **2 Hard disk** – an input and output device, used for holding megabytes or gigabytes of information. Nowadays hard disks fit inside the control unit's box – unlike the first hard disk. When it appeared in 1956, it was twice the size of a refrigerator! (Maybe that's why everybody thought it was such a cool device!)

▶ **3 Diskette unit** – also an input and output device, it takes a diskette which usually holds less than 1.5 Mb of information. It's one you can take out and carry around in your pocket, though, because it's the size of a biscuit in a flat case. Top tip: do not confuse the two! Diskettes do not like being dunked in cups of tea!

▶ **4 CD ROM drive** – takes a round, flat, shiny disk which can hold 680 Mb of data. Because of this, it's perfect for sound and pictures, which take a lot of space and won't fit on a diskette. CD-ROMs also last a lot longer. Tests have shown that a CD should last for at least 50 years ... and if it's well kept, could hang on for 400 million!

▶ **5 Keyboard** – A board, with keys! Hit one and the appropriate character is input to the computer. Can't find the right key? Then blame history. The layout, named "QWERTY" after the top row of letter keys, dates from the earliest typewriters. It was designed so that the letters used most often were right under a touch-typist's eight fingers. Not a lot of help if you only use one!

▶ **6 Mouse** – an input device used to move a pointer (called a *cursor*) round the screen. Clicking the mouse button is also a simple "input", which tells the computer to make a note of the new position. The mouse, so called because of its shape and the "tail" of cable connecting it to the computer, was invented in 1970. The first models had wooden shells and slid around on two metal wheels.

▶ **7 VDU (*Visual Display Unit*)** – the major output device, used to display everything from words to moving pictures. Some people say that staring at a VDU all day can strain your eyes. If they're right, then maybe the letters should stand for Very Dodgy Unit!

▶ **8 Printer** – The next major output device, used to present results on paper in either black and white or colour. It's also the oldest of all the devices. A printer was part of Charles Babbage's designs in 1833!

▶ **9 Speaker** – Outputs sounds, from the roar of a crowd to a blood-curdling scream.

Crashing hardware fact

Not every piece of hardware is vitally important, though. A 1980's make of computer called the Amstrad PC1512 had a lot of failures reported. This led to the rumour that, because it didn't have a cooling fan like other PC's, it was overheating. Amstrad's owner, Alan Sugar, argued that his computer didn't need a fan. (Fans keep the power supply in the control unit cool, but the PC1512's power supply wasn't in the control unit). But the rumours continued and sales started to fall. How did Sugar solve the problem? He changed his PC's design to include a useless, but loud and whirry, fan – and sales boomed again!

Software

Software is the name given to all the programs computers obey. It's mysterious stuff because, unlike hardware, you can't see software – rather like electricity, or the juices and gunge that worked on the food in Og the Caveman's stomach. You know the software's around because of the results it produces!

Authors write books, poets write poems, teachers write reports, Batman and Robin right wrongs – and computer programmers write computer programs. This activity, called *programming*, is a complicated business (which is why computer programmers get paid plenty of money!) but here are the main steps:

FIG 1:

FIG 2:

FIG 3:

1 Design the program. This involves drawing up a plan to show everything the computer's got to do.
2 Write the program by turning your plan into a list of instructions written in a special language called a programming language. (You have to learn this language first. It's a bit like learning a foreign language. Ooh, la la!)
3 Convert your program into binary code. (Don't worry, programmers don't have to do this! It's all done by another type of program

44

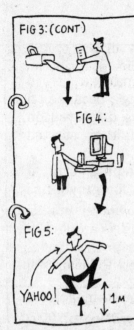

FIG 3: (CONT)

FIG 4:

FIG 5:

YAHOO!

1M

called a translator program which inputs instructions written in a programming language and outputs them in binary. How do translators get translated? Don't ask!)

4 Load your program into the computer and test it.

5 If it works shout "Yahoo!" and do twenty handsprings. If it fails, go back to step 1 and work out what you've forgotten – and keep doing so until your program does work!

As you can see, the hard part is step 1. Miss out a vital instruction and you'll have a crashing computer!

But thinking of every step the computer's got to follow is really difficult, even for quite simple programs – such as those which control tamagotchi pets. Yes, those friendly Japanese toys are little computers, with programs which *input* from the toy's buttons and *output* to its display. In between, the *processing* follows a set of rules.

What sort of rules? That depends on the type of pet. Some tamagotchis are dogs. Some are cats. Some are aliens. Let's be different. Let's imagine you've got...

A Tamagotchi teacher!

Crashing Tamagotchi facts

▶ *Tamagotchi* is a Japanese word meaning "lovable little egg", because an egg is what the first toys displayed on their little screens when they started up.

▶ Millions of Japanese adults own a tamagotchi. It was a toy for grown-ups first! Attached to a key ring, it reminded them where their car and door keys were!

▶ Over 50 million tamagotchis have been sold worldwide.

▶ In the early days, when tamagotchis were hard to get hold of, people who'd bought one for £10 were able to sell it for £500. Now you can get them for £2!

As with any tamagotchi pet, in this game owners will have to press buttons to "care" for their darling little teacher whenever it calls attention. The aim will be to keep Sir or Miss going for a whole term of 100 days

So, what sort of caring will a tamagotchi teacher need? Other cyber-pets call for food, but let's have our teacher calling for something much more likely: a cup of tea! Instead of a cuddle, let's have them wanting a really loud shout. And instead of a trip to the loo ... no, forget the instead of. With all that tea-drinking, a trip to the loo is what a tamagotchi teacher will need too!

This could be the teacher's timetable of events for any one day:.

0830	Have a cup of tea
0900	Shout at class
1055	Go to the loo
1100	Have a cup of tea
1200	Scream at class
1255	Go to the loo
1300	Have a cup of tea
1330	Bellow at class
1425	Go to the loo
1430	Have a cup of tea
1530	Cheer!

There will be certain rules that have to be followed by the program as well:

▶ Teachers start with a "life" of 100 days.
▶ If they're given their vital cup of tea within 10 minutes of calling for it then they're refreshed; if not their life shortens by one day.
▶ If they're taken to the loo within five minutes they're happy; if not their life is shortened by two days for disgracing themselves.
▶ If they're allowed to shout, scream and bellow within one minute they're delighted; if not, they lose five days off their life (which shows how important a good roar is to a teacher's health).
▶ If their life goes down to zero then they're sent home on sick leave!

So, how would the program work? What steps would it have to follow? Here's a diagram for the first event of the day.

SET LIFE = 100 DAYS : A "counter" for how long the teacher's got to live!

LIFE = 100 DAYS

8:30 CUP OF TEA

INPUT THE TIME OF DAY: The computer's clock is inspected. Different sections of the program are obeyed depending on the time of day

IS IT 8:30 ?:

If the answer is no, then the program will go on and look for all the other times in the timetable. If none of them match it will input the time again and keep doing it until a time does match.

SOUND A BEEP: Two outputs

"BEEP! BEEP!"

HAS THE TEA BUTTON BEEN PRESSED YET? The owner should now "give" the thirsty teacher a cup of tea by pressing the right button, when DISPLAY the program receives this input A TEA CUP

it goes back to looking for another important time. If the owner is asleep... or doing something else...

LOO

ZZZ

HA! HA!

(or maybe just wanting to make their tamagotchi teacher suffer!)

Then the input won't arrive...

WAITING MORE THAN 10 MINUTES FOR THE TEA BUTTON TO BE PRESSED?

By checking the time the program will workout how long it's been waiting. When the time is up, that event has been missed...

REDUCE LIFE BY ONE DAY!

Which means for a missed cup of tea the teacher's life goes down by one day!

GO BACK TO INPUT THE TIME OF DAY AGAIN...

Having dealt with the 0830 event, the program would now go back and wait for the next time to arrive. This is called a program "loop"...

NO CUP OF TEA IN THE MORNING IS DEFINITELY LOOPY!

Apart from the first step (it wouldn't make sense to put the teacher's life back to 100 every time something happened!) all the events would be pretty similar. At 0900 the program calls for the teacher to be given a shout, at 1055 to be taken to the loo, and so on.

49

Have you spotted the deliberate mistake, though? It's one of these three – but which one?

a The teacher would live for ever.

b The teacher would ask for a cup of tea every 10 minutes.

c A real tamagotchi teacher would ask for green tea.

Answer: a – Although the teacher's life is being shortened there's no step in the program to check when it's got down to zero so that s/he can be packed off on sick leave. As it stands, the program would carry on even when the LIFE counter went down to lower than zero. Your teacher would live for ever!

That's an example of how errors get into computer programs. Sometimes they're small errors, sometimes they're silly – and sometimes they're totally crashing! Read on for some examples that are as bad. (OK, so nothing could be as bad as an everlasting teacher. Some examples that are *nearly* as bad then!)

Big Money, Big Mistakes

Sometimes computers crash and sometimes they go wrong. Sometimes, though, they never work at all. Like the 1970's computer system that was supposed to be installed in a spy plane called the Nimrod...

What would you do?

Nimrod was a computer system that crashed before it was put into action. Others have gone wrong much later – when they were supposed be working!

Here's a quick quiz about three of these computers. If you'd been there, could you have stopped what happened?

Calling all martians!

You're told you're going to be the person in charge of sending commands to the computer controlling a Russian spacecraft on its way to Mars. What do you do?

a Learn Russian.

b Learn to type accurately.

c Learn astronomy.

Answer – b. When the operator sent some commands to alter the spacecraft's direction, he made a single typing mistake. This caused the computer to spin the spacecraft around so that its solar panels no longer faced the sun. By the time the mistake was discovered the craft's batteries had gone flat and it couldn't be controlled any more. It was lost in space!

Emergency!

It's 1992 and you're an ambulance driver in London. A new computer system has been brought in, and it tells you to follow a particular route through to where you're needed. You know a short cut, though, that will get you there quicker. What should you do?

a Follow the computer's route.

b Take your short cut.

c Ask a policeman the best way to go.

Answer – a. You should follow the computer's route. That way it will know where your ambulance is, and be able to send you to a different place in an emergency. Unfortunately, some of the drivers went for answer b. They also made mistakes when reporting back their positions. Worse still, the equipment kept going wrong and so did the software. Eventually the computer's map was so muddled it didn't know where anything was. As it tried to sort itself out, the system became so overloaded that it stopped emergency calls getting through.

Scramble!

It's 1:26 am on 3 June 1980. You're in charge of the control room at the Strategic Air Command post near Omaha, Nebraska in the USA. Suddenly one of your displays flashes up a warning that two missiles are heading your way! What do you do?

a Tell your bomber crews to get ready and have your own missiles prepared for launching.

b Wait for a minute and see what happens.

Answer – b. Trouble is, after waiting for a minute your display changes again to show that even more missiles are coming! Now what do you do?

a Tell your bomber crews to get ready and have your own missiles prepared for launching.

b Wait for a few more minutes and see what happens.

Answer – a. But while everybody's getting ready the displays change again. This time they say there aren't any missiles coming after all! Now what do you do?

a Panic and start World War III.

b Dive under the table and hold your ears.

c Call an engineer to look the computer.

Answer – a bit of a, a bit of b, but mostly c.
A panicky round table meeting between top Generals decided that the computer's warnings were a false alarm. To their great relief, they were right. When the engineer arrived he found that a chip had failed and started displaying a random test message!

Who are you calling a failure?
Why do computers crash? Why do they make mistakes? Aren't they tested first?

Yes, they are. But sometimes it isn't the program that's wrong – it's the person using it...

The sick sick note

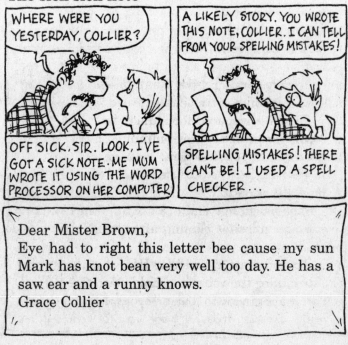

WHERE WERE YOU YESTERDAY, COLLIER?

OFF SICK, SIR. LOOK, I'VE GOT A SICK NOTE. ME MUM WROTE IT USING THE WORD PROCESSOR ON HER COMPUTER

A LIKELY STORY. YOU WROTE THIS NOTE, COLLIER. I CAN TELL FROM YOUR SPELLING MISTAKES!

SPELLING MISTAKES! THERE CAN'T BE! I USED A SPELL CHECKER...

Dear Mister Brown,
Eye had to right this letter bee cause my sun Mark has knot bean very well too day. He has a saw ear and a runny knows.
Grace Collier

What went wrong? Nothing. A spell checker works by comparing the words it receives against a big list of the words it's been told about. Because every word in Collier's sick note is a proper word, none of them were marked as spelling mistakes!

Plenty of real mistakes are made by computer programs, even though they're tested carefully. The problem is that the bigger a program gets, the harder it is to test every little bit of it. In fact, even quite small problems can be very difficult to test...

Which Way Now?

"Right, Watts," said Mr Thyke, the senior maths master. "It's a practical maths lesson for you today. You're going orienteering."

Tarquin Watts had special lessons on his own because he was so bright. That's why they called him Mega Watts.

"Orienteering? Is that an activity which originated in the Orient?"

"I don't know, and I don't care. You aren't going that far anyway. You're just going out of the school gates and across to the park. Being a dedicated chap, I've already been there this morning..."

Mega flicked an eyebrow skywards. "There's no point in me going then, is there? You can tell me what it was like."

"You're not going there to see what it's like, Watts! You're going there to find twelve markers I've put out. Here's a map showing where they are. For your special maths exercise today, I want you to work out the shortest route between them."

"Between all twelve?" said Mega.

"Yes, yes, all twelve. They're an average of 50 metres apart. That's only 600 metres in total, Watts. You should be able to get round them all in five minutes. Try all the possible routes, then come back and see me when you've finished."

Mega shook his head. "Sorry, sir. I won't be able to do that."

"What, Watts? Why not?"

"Because I'll be dead, Mr Thyke. And so will you. What you've asked me to do will take 4,557 years and 260 days!"

How come? Because the number of possible routes is huge! Mega's first marker could be in any one of 12 places. His second marker could be any one of the remaining 11. So to try all the possibilities for just the first two markers would mean 12 times $11 = 132$ tries. To continue the problem and try all the possible routes round the whole twelve markers would mean

$$12 \times 11 \times 10 \times 9 \times 8 \times 7 \times 6 \times 5 \times 4 \times 3 \times 2 \times 1 =$$
$$479,001,600 \text{ routes.}$$

Mega's estimate came from working out how long all those would take to do at 5 minutes per route. (Non-stop, that is. If he had a sleep it would take longer!)

This is the sort of problem that crops up when testing complicated computer programs with billions of different "routes" through them. Because it's impossible to test all the routes, programmers test as many as they can. Crashes occur when the program is sent down a route that hasn't been tested.

Wobbling around the world

It's this difficulty of testing absolutely everything that cause many computers to crash – or, if not crash, wobble very badly! Often the problem has a very simple explanation. So, fancy yourself as a cracker of crashing conundrums? Then see if you can work out what went wrong with this set of worldwide wobblers!

1 A parcel found at a post office in Nagano, Japan, was beeping suspiciously. The police who raced to the scene thought they'd found a computer-controlled bomb. They hadn't. What had they found?

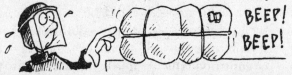

2 Another police problem, this time in Scotland. When all the computer screens went blank at Crastonhill Police Office, in Glasgow, the officers suspected foul play – until the expert called to help them with their enquiries uncovered the cause of the trouble. What was it?

3 In Brazil in 1994, twins and triplets discovered they weren't allowed to vote in the elections – by order of a computer! Why not?

4 The driver of a US Army lorry was surprised to find he couldn't pay for his lunch using his credit card. Why not?

5 In March 1997, every train in southern Finland was halted by a paper clip. How?

6 In the UK, a British Gas computer sent out a letter to thousands of customers telling them that their gas would be cut off because they hadn't paid their bills – which was true. But why hadn't they paid them?

7 In 1988 an Australian computer nearly drowned a newspaper editor. How?

8 In Holland a chemical plant exploded in 1992 causing several deaths – and it was all down to a wrongly typed comma. What was the problem?

9 In 1995, Sonny Walker, a 19-year-old Canadian, was watching a TV crime programme showing the faces of suspects ... when up onto the screen popped his own face! Why?

COME OUT WITH YOUR HANDS UP!

10 A computer-controlled factory in New Zealand was shut down on 31 December 1996 for a holiday.

What should have happened?

controlling computers so that the space bar wouldn't work. This stopped the computer, which stopped the trains!

6 Because the computer hadn't sent the bills out yet!

7 The computer was used to calculate the times of high and low tides which were printed in the Australian newspaper *The Canberra Times*. Unfortunately they were wrong – as the editor discovered when he was swept out to sea! When he got back he quickly made sure it didn't happen again, though. *The Canberra Times* was his newspaper!

8 Commas were used to show decimal places in numbers. The mistakenly-placed comma caused the computer which controlled the mixing of chemicals to use the wrong amounts.

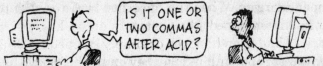

9 Walker was unlucky enough to withdraw some money from a bank's cash machine one hour after somebody else had used a stolen credit card at the same machine. But the camera's clock was one hour slow, so the credit card fraud was matched with his photograph – a mistake not discovered until his face had been flashed around Canada!

10 It should have stayed open and shut down the next day, January! The problem was that 1996 was a leap year and the computer had been programmed wrongly. It didn't count the extra day and shut down 24 hours too soon!

THESE ARE THE BEST COMPUTER ERRORS

Stop bugging me!

As the New Zealand problem in the wobbling around the world quiz showed, computers have trouble with dates. Here are a couple more examples. What have they both got in common?

1 In 1996 a car hire company bought a batch of new cars. The details were logged on their computer with a note saying they were to be sold when they were four years old. The computer immediately replied that the cars should be sold at once, for £10 each!

2 In 1995 the computer control system at Marks and Spencer rejected batches of corned beef even though it had a shelf-life of five years.

Answer: What they have in common is something known as the "Millennium Bug", an error which makes computers take the year 2000 as 1900 instead! So...

1 When the car hire computer worked out the sell-by-date for the new cars it came up with the year 1900 – making it think they were already 96 years old and well past it! That's why it said they should be sold at once.

2 The corned beef became scorned beef for the same

reason. The Marks and Spencers computer thought it had been in its cans for 95 years!

Crashing fact

Software problems were first called "bugs" in the 1940's. Grace Hopper, a USA Navy lieutenant, was working on one of the earliest computers when it suddenly stopped. Finding a moth trapped in one of the machine's moving parts, she reported: "Computer failure caused by bug"!

The car hire and corned beef problems occurred because the programs were designed only to store the *year* part of the date and not the century. So the year "1984" would have been stored as just "84" and the century part thrown away.

That's the problem with the year 2000. Throw away the century part and you get "00" – which any computer software that hasn't been updated would do one of two things with...

▶ think the date must be wrong – and stop!
▶ or, worse, think the date is fine ... and it's the year 1900!

Why did programmers use this dozy scheme? Because when they were writing the software, as long ago as the 1960s in some cases, computer memory was expensive and any trick that could save some was used. Besides, none of them expected their software still to be around in the year 2000!

But – what if it lasts even longer...

Dateline: 1 JANUARY 2999
From: PEARL E. GATES, SUPREME
**   PRESIDENT, PLANET EARTH**
To: ALL COMPUTER PROGRAMMERS

Hi! And a happy New Year! We're now just twelve months away from a really important date – and I don't mean the 975th anniversary of my great ancestor Bill Gates finally collecting enough money to buy the whole world. Nope, I'm talking about the new millennium. The year 3000!

That's why I'm writing this memo. According to papers in a time capsule we opened up the other day, the last millennium back in year 2000 caused a few computer problems. Before it arrived they were predicting stacks of them:

▶ bank and credit card computers charging 100 years of interest

▶ aeroplanes not even taking off because the booking computers thought that they're going to arrive (in 1900) before they've left (in 1999)

▶ telegrams from the Queen congratulating new-born babies on their 100th birthdays

▶ computerized equipment of all sorts simply stopping because it thought it had been working for 100 years without being checked – equipment like jumbo jets, heart monitors, security cameras, traffic lights, fire alarms, video recorders, motorway signs, petrol pumps, vending machines, supermarket tills...

Of course, not all of the predictions came true. But some of them did, and I'm counting on all you programmers to make sure this millennium goes off without a hitch. I don't want to see any of the heart-rending little notes from schoolkids we found in that year 2000 capsule. Notes like this one –

My New Year

I had a rotten New year. Really rotten. My birthday was on 1 January so Dad went to the bank to get some money out. He couldn't have any! The computer in the bank's safe thought the date had gone backwards. As that wasn't right it had locked the doors - to be on the "safe" side, the manager said, "Ha-ha, very funny." I didn't think so cos I didn't get my pressie!

Meg A. Byte

Let's have none of that in the year 3000, folks. If a doting Dad wants to buy his young 'un a birthday yo-yo, I want you to make sure he can get his £1 million out to pay for it!

MY NEW Year

I got banned from using the telephone! Just before midnight I thought I'd ring my friend to wish her a happy 2000. Next day we got cut off! The phone company computer had got

its dates wrong. It thought I'd started
talking in 1900. Kept going for 99 years - and
not paid the bill!
     •.. Watt A Mess

I don't want to see stories like this, either. If
youngsters want to vidi-call their little alien
chums on Alpha Centauri, then let's have 'em
do it without a problem. Same goes for party-
going...

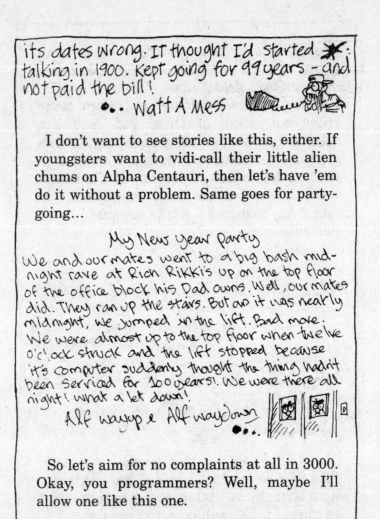

My New Year Party

We and our mates went to a big bash midnight rave at Rich Rikki's up on the top floor
of the office block his Dad owns. Well, our mates
did. They ran up the stairs. But as it was nearly
midnight, we jumped in the lift. Bad move.
We were almost up to the top floor when twelve
o'clock struck and the lift stopped because
it's computer suddenly thought the thing hadn't
been serviced for 100 years! We were there all
night! What a let down!

     Alf wayup & Alf waydown •..

So let's aim for no complaints at all in 3000.
Okay, you programmers? Well, maybe I'll
allow one like this one.

MY NEW YEAR ..·

I HATE COMPUTER PROGRAMMERS! COMPUTER
PROGRAMMERS . FIXED THE SCHOOL COMPUTER
AND I DIDN'T WANT THEM TO TOUCH IT! I WANTED
IT LEFT ALONE, SO IT WOULD THINK IT WAS 1900
INSTEAD OF 2000. THAT WAY IT WOULD HAVE

THOUGHT I WAS 89 AND NOT 11! THEN IT WOULD
HAVE SENT ME A LETTER SAYING IT WAS TIME I
LEFT SCHOOL! AND I WOULD! FAST! I HATE
COMPUTER PROGRAMMERS! LES E. BONES

You've spotted my little joke, of course! We won't see a letter like that in 3000 because now that everybody lives to be 600 they all stay at school until they're 90 anyway!

So, do your job, programmers. No millennium bugs! Let's make 3000 a year to remember!

Crashing fact
Watch out for 31 December 2000! That's another dodgy date because 2000 is an "uncommon" leap year (years ending in 00 but divisible by 4 usually aren't leap years). So programs that haven't been set up to treat 2000 as a leap year may not crash until the end of December, when they discover the year is one day longer than expected!

"Crushing" computers!
It doesn't matter when it happens, though – if your computer crashes then you've got problems. What do you do?

Call an engineer?

That's what they did at a missile base in the USSR when a complicated and expensive guidance computer went down in 1986. According to a report in the *Weekly World News*, though, it was the worst thing they could have done. The engineer who arrived was just that – a man used to fixing engines!

After poking around for a bit in one of the VDU's, he decided that something must be stuck.

His solution? Squirt oil into it!

Result? Every circuit in the control centre blew up and it took six weeks to put it all back together again! (Long after the engineer had sidled away saying something like, "oil be off, then…")

"Fix" it yourself

In July 1997, a man living in Washington decided he could do what was wanted himself. He'd got so annoyed with his PC crashing that he "fixed" it good and proper – by pumping four bullets into its case and finishing it off with another one through the VDU screen!

Attack! Attack!

A woman peace campaigner took similarly drastic action in 1988, but on a much bigger scale. She launched her own attack against a $1billion computer she thought was being built to launch an attack against Russia. Using a crowbar, hammer, cordless drill, bolt-cutter and a fire extinguisher, she managed to wreck it. In return, the court hammered her: she was jailed for 5 years and fined $500,000.

If at first you don't succeed...

But what on earth could make a writer named Stephen Manes want to do this to his portable computer in 1997?

- ▶ kick it
- ▶ drop it while it was saving a file
- ▶ throw on the pavement
- ▶ drown it in water and cola
- ▶ jump on it
- ▶ reverse over it in his car.

Answer: He was testing it! The manufacturer claimed the computer was accident proof and he was writing an article about it for a magazine. What's more, the computer passed the test. Apart from a few scratches and a squeaky handle it carried on working! (Note: *Do not try this on your school computers!*)

Tasty!

Finally, you could always do what Frenchman Michel Lotto did – and eat your computer! Why did he do it? Not because he was frustrated, but because he had a taste for eating odd things. Over the years had tucked into 18 bicycles, 15 supermarket trollies, seven TV sets, six chandeliers, two beds and a small aeroplane! So why a computer? He must have heard that they contained lots of bytes!

Here, There and Everywhere

Computers don't crash that often – and a good job too. They're in so many places nowadays that if they kept on conking out, the whole world would grind to a halt.

So, do you think you're switched on when it comes to the jobs computers are doing today? Reckon you can tell when a computer's chugging away behind the scenes? Then input your answers to this True/False quiz and see what sort of score you compute!

1 In the UK, Thames Trains have a computer-controlled train which refuses to move if it's too cold. **True or False?**

2 A computer has been used to judge a beauty contest – with men *and* women contestants pitted against each other! **True or False?**

3 In Macy's department store in New York, a computer helps customers try on swimsuits. **True or False?**

I ONLY WANTED A BEACH TOWEL!

4 If you find an unexploded bomb in your back garden, bomb disposal experts will turn up with a computer which tells them what to do.
True or False?

5 In an experiment, 600 plaice were fitted with microchips and released into North Sea – and any fisherman catching one given a £500 reward!
True or False?

6 If you don't want a job in which you have to use a computer you should become a traffic warden.
True or False?

COULD YOU WAIT FIVE MINUTES WHILE I TYPE THIS UP?

7 Police on murder hunts are using a computer to turn a photograph of a victim into a skeleton.
True or False?

8 Every registered horse in Ireland has to have a microchip inserted in its neck. **True or False?**

9 In August 1998, a computer stopped a Runaway Train at Disneyland in Paris. **True or False?**

LUCKY THE TRAIN STOPPED, OR YOU'D HAVE BEEN A DEAD DUCK!

10 Computers devise fitness programs for cows. **True or False?**

Answers:

1 FALSE – but their trains do have a computer-controlled system which sprinkles sand on icy rails so that they can run in cold weather

I BET YOU'LL BE GLAD WHEN THIS COMPUTER'S FIXED ?

2 TRUE. The contest wasn't judged on the sizes of bumpy bits, though. It was based on the notion that beautiful faces are symmetrical – that is, both eyes are the same distance from the nose and so on. Measurements of the contestant's faces were input and the computer worked out which face was the winner.

3 TRUE. The computer puts the swimsuit on a model matching the customer's own shape and displays the picture on a screen.

4 TRUE. It will have a CD-ROM showing the details of the hundreds of different types of bomb there are and how to make them safe. Because bombs are often badly rusted, the system can also try to identify the bomb and give advise on what to do from any details available.

5 FALSE. The reward was only £25. The rest of the story is true, though. The aim was to find out how the fish moved around, so that fisherman would know where best to find them.

6 FALSE. Traffic wardens use hand-held computers to take car numbers and print out parking tickets.

7 FALSE. It works the other way round. If they find a mystery skeleton, police can use a program which will show them what the person's face looked like when they were alive. Or, if they suspect that the person is somebody in particular, can match that person's face against the skull.

8 TRUE. The chip identifies the horse's owner and can be used to track them down if the horse runs away.

9 TRUE. Computers monitor what's happening on theme park rides and control the speed at which they travel. If any problems are detected, the ride shuts down – which is what happened with the

"Runaway Train" ride at Disneyland in Paris. It was halted just as before the train hurtled down through a tunnel. The passengers weren't too relieved, though. They had to hang on at the top of a canyon for 20 minutes!

10 FALSE. But they do devise personal menus for them! Dairies are now putting micro-chip tags on to their cows to identify them to a computer which records the feed it's given, how much milk it produces, how creamy it is – and various other moooving facts!

How did you get on?
10 out of 10: You don't need a computer, you've already got a brain like one.
4–9: With a bit of reprogramming you could be pretty switched on.
Less than 4: Sure you haven't had your memory wiped clean?

Cruising computer fact
Runners in the London Marathon wear a "Championchip" microchip attached to their running shoes. Whenever they cross one of the special mats dotted all along the course, the chip sends a signal back to a computer so that it can keep track of who the athlete is and how far they've got. When they cross the finishing line the computer records their time and when the race is over it prints a result list. How? By "running" its program, of course!

My computer's watching you!

As the "Here, there and everywhere" quiz shows, computers are being used in all sorts of ways. But just because they *can* be used to do many different things, does it follow that they always *have* to be?

Sounds like just the sort of investigation for a world-famous detective...

The mysterious case of the supermarket shopper's secrets

Dr Watson eased himself out of his chair and walked over to the other side of the Baker Street room to see what his good friend Sherlock Holmes was doing on his computer. "Holmes, my dear fellow, if you sit in front of that computer for much longer you'll get square eyes."

Sherlock Holmes looked away from the screen briefly. "One must move with the times, Watson. I am simply researching our current case."

"The Case of the Teacher and her Obnoxious Jam-Covered Pupil?" gasped Watson. "The teacher who accompanied that rude little boy in here late Friday afternoon, the boy who demanded

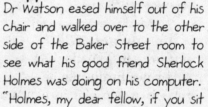

that you find out who attacked him at the end of the lunch break, covered him in strawberry jam and left him in the school conservation area no more than five metres away from a wasp nest?"

"Miss Exhausted and Augustus Whinge," nodded Holmes. "The very teacher and the very pupil."

Watson snorted. "I have to say, Holmes, that if Whinge had been my pupil it would have been me who carried out the deed!"

"A suspicion that I immediately entertained of Miss Exhausted," said Sherlock Holmes.

"Which is why I asked her the question I did. Can you remember it?"

"Perfectly," said Dr Watson. "You asked her if she possessed a supermarket shopper's card."

"To which she answered?"

"Yes, she did. But how that knowledge is of assistance to you is beyond me, Holmes."

The great detective made a final note from the information displayed on his VDU, saved his work, then turned off his computer with a flourish.

"All is about to be revealed, Watson." Holmes peeled his pad back through page after page of closely-spaced writing. "But first, look for yourself. Here are a few things I have discovered about our Miss Exhausted."

Name: Patience Exhausted

Date of Birth: 20 February 1971

Ocupation: Teacher

Does her main weekly shopping every friday between the hours of 12 noon and 1 pm.

Drives a small clean car.

Reads the Daily Moon newspaper.

Owns a dog.

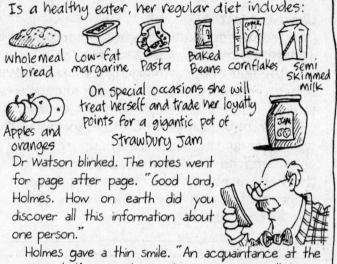

Is a healthy eater, her regular diet includes:

wholemeal bread   Low-fat margarine   Pasta   Baked Beans   cornflakes   semi skimmed milk

Apples and oranges

On special occasions she will treat herself and trade her loyalty points for a gigantic pot of Strawbury Jam

Dr Watson blinked. The notes went for page after page. "Good Lord, Holmes. How on earth did you discover all this information about one person."

Holmes gave a thin smile. "An acquaintance at the supermarket's computer centre owed me a small favour – so I asked for a copy of Miss Exhausted's file."

"You mean ... whenever anybody ... me, even ... uses one of those cards to build up some points for little luxuries at Christmas – information about me is sent to a computer?"

"Most definitely, Watson. The fact that you like to wear Mr Men underpants is without doubt logged on a computer somewhere."

"I don't think we need to go into that! But, tell me ... these facts about Miss Exhausted. Are they held on just one computer?"

"Just one," said Holmes seriously. "Along with similar facts for at least 7 million other shoppers. Facts that, with a little bit of deduction, reveal a great deal about the person concerned – as I will demonstrate in the case of Miss Exhausted ..."

Crashing fact

One supermarket chain's computer apparently revealed that a large number of late-night shoppers buying nappies also bought beer. Deciding that these shoppers must be men who'd been sent out by their wives to buy nappies and then stocked up with beer at the same time, supermarket chiefs moved the beer section nearer to the baby section. That way, they hoped, more babies and dads could suck their bottles together!

(continued)

The detective then went through his list, tapping each item as he referred to it.

"Name, occupation and date of birth all have to be supplied when applying for a shopper's card. Then, whenever it's used, date and time of day are stored. In this way a pattern of movement can be built up. That is how I know that she usually shops at Friday lunchtimes."

"And was Miss Exhausted in the supermarket on the Friday in question? Surely she has a perfect alibi if she was."

"She was, Watson. But, to continue. The lady regularly buys petrol on her arrival. Not a large amount, which suggests she owns a small car. She also pays to use the car wash, which causes me to deduce that it is a clean car."

"Amazing, Holmes!"

"Her regular purchases include the healthy items you see listed, together with the *Daily Moon* newspaper and some tins of *Doggie-Dins*."

"Hence, also, your knowledge about her reading habits and pet ownership!" Watson shook his head in wonder.

"Now," said Sherlock Holmes, "we come to the nub of the matter. Although Miss Exhausted is a healthy eater, the computer records show that she occasionally succumbs to temptation and purchases strawberry jam in large quantities."

"The records show that?"

"Indeed, Watson. Any item which appears frequently over a period of months will be considered by the supermarket to be a regular purchase. By a process of elimination, therefore, those items that a shopper might deem luxuries can be identified."

"Extra-large jars of strawberry jam, in Miss Exhausted's case."

 "Correct. And, having identified such items, the supermarket will endeavour to tempt the shopper by offering extra loyalty points on that item."

"And were extra points being offered for giant jams on Friday, Holmes?"

"They were!"

"Things are starting to look sticky for Miss Exhausted," said Dr Watson slowly. "But – no! Did you not say she was in the supermarket at the hour when the dreadful Augustus Whinge was smeared?"

The great detective pointed at one final piece of

information. At the bottom of the list was a time.

"Miss Exhausted passed through the supermarket at 12:52 on Friday last, Watson. Leaving her time enough to return to school and put Whinge into the jam of which he has complained."

"Brilliant, Holmes! And all deduced from information held on a computer about every shopper."

"Quite true," sighed Holmes. "Another case solved."

"But ... why do you sigh, man? Once again you have shown that your powers of deduction are second to none."

Sherlock Holmes shook his head seriously. "On the contrary, Watson. With the information they are collecting, supermarket managers are doing exactly what I have done – but for every one of their customers."

"Good Lord, Holmes!"

"You are right to be shocked, Watson. For make no mistake about it. We are becoming a land, not of supermarkets, but of *snoopermarkets!*"

"We know how frequently our customers shop, the ages of their children and whether they have a cat or a dog or a budgie" – Director of a Supermarket

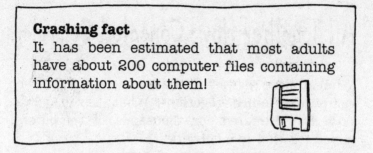
Any organization can keep facts about you on their computer – and you can't stop them! The law says they can do it, so long as they tell somebody called the Data Protection Registrar that they're keeping personal data on their computer. The law also says that companies (but not the police) must tell you what information they're keeping about you. There's only one snag. In order to find out, you've got to pay a fee! Sounds more like a data protection racket!

All Together Now! Conected Computers

What's more powerful than a computer? Two computers joined together! What's even more powerful? Hundreds or thousands of computers joined together in a network.

When the network works, of course...

82

The idea behind computer networking is that information from one computer can be sent to another – without mistakes! (unlike Major Blood-Boyle's message). It's a very powerful feature, especially when the computers aren't simply in the same building, but dotted all around the world.

Scope for even bigger crashes, you might think! Quite the opposite. As this timeline shows, computer networking was actually invented to guard against crashes – very big crashes...

Computer networks timeline

1960s The first network is set up to link together military computers across the USA. The thinking is that even if one of the computers is flattened by a bomb (not to mention the building it's in, and the city the building's in) it will just be a case of linking to another computer in the network.

1970s The system is so successful that universities in the USA network their computers so that they can exchange research results (and play a multi-user computer game called *Dungeons and Dragons*!). Soon universities in other countries are doing the same thing. (They want to play the game too!)

1980s Networks become networked! Computers in different countries can now talk to each other (and play international *Dungeons and Dragons*!) This set up becomes known as *The Internet*. Using it isn't simple, though. It's like having a telephone but no telephone directory – you can only call a computer if you already know its address.

1990s Fed up with this Tim Berners-Lee, a research worker at the Swiss company CERN, designs a *browser* program called Mosaic. It's like using a computer version of the Yellow Pages; give the program a topic and it searches the network for anything about it. The whole global network gets a new name: the World-Wide Web.

2000s How will the World-Wide Web grow? Very quickly by the look of it! In

1997 the Internet had an estimated size of 4 million computers within 30,000 linked networks – and there were 38 million users!

Crashing fact

Researchers were surprised to discover that the number of users connected to the Internet dropped dramatically at the same time every week – until they looked at the TV listings and saw that the fall coincided with the time *The X-Files* came on.

The incredible Internet

Connecting to the Internet is to enter another world. You can "visit" different locations, known as *web sites* (just as you might visit somebody's home) either through knowing their *web address* or by discovering them while surfing.

Let's say you want to pay an electronic visit to Queen Elizabeth II. Easy. The Queen's always at home on the Net! The address of the Royal Family's web site is:

www.royal.gov.uk

ER... I DON'T THINK THEY HAVE A CORGI WEB SITE, MUMMY

Zip to this site and you can tour the royal palaces, find out about the history of the royal family and much more. The address may look weird, but the different parts (the bits separated by stops) all mean something ...

▶ **www** – short for world-wide web, says that this is a web site rather than any other type of site.

▶ **royal** – tells you the site's owner

▶ **gov** – is a wider group name short for "government", because that's what the royal family are part of. Other common group names are "co" or "com" for "company".

▶ **uk** – the widest group name of the lot, this says which country the web site is in. Every country in the world has its own two letter code – except for one. Because the Internet began in the USA, adding a country code to all their addresses would have been a big job. So they have a no-letter code! A web address without a country code is American.

Addresses can become a lot more complicated, especially if they're pointing you deeper into a web site. For instance, how about signing the Royal Family's visitor's book? Just tack a little more onto the end of their web site address and you'll be there:

www.royal.gov.uk/vbk/index.htm

That's the great thing about the Internet. You can visit places that you'd never get to in any other way. Like…

▶ The White House, in Washington. No need to put up with all the hassle of being President. Just visit the address –
http://www.whitehouse.gov/WH/Welcome. html for a guided tour.

▶ No. 10 Downing Street, in London. Don't bother about getting elected and fighting your way through parliament. Type in –
www.number-10.gov.uk/index.html for a look round. You'll even be invited to join a discussion group to say what you think the government should be doing. ("Pay pupils for going to school!" "If uniforms are so good, why don't teachers wear them!")

Serious surfing!
"Surfing the Net" – that is, jumping from one site to

88

another as the fancy takes you – is simple. What's more, you don't get wet! It's all done by using nifty things called *hypertext links*.

These are underlined words or phrases in the page you're looking at. Click on one and it's like bouncing on a springboard. You'll jump off to another place! But remember, the net's not free. There could be big bills to pay if you use it a lot.

So, try some paper net-surfing with the game on the next page and see if you can match the web-site descriptions with the underlined words on the computer screen. Get them all right, and you're a serious surfer. All wrong ... and you're a pathetic plunger!

The Internet Game ⟶

1. NEED TO SEND A BIRTHDAY CARD? USE THE NET. THERE ARE SITES THAT WILL LET YOU DESIGN YOUR OWN CARD. THEY'LL THEN PRINT IT AND PUT IT IN THE POST FOR YOU! IN THE FUTURE CARDS WILL DISAPPEAR ACCORDING TO SOME PEOPLE. IN A SURVEY, 43% THOUGHT THEY'D BE SENDING ELECTRONIC GREETINGS BY 2000. NOT A LOT OF GOOD IF YOUR GRANNIE ISN'T ON LINE!

2. WANT TO KNOW IF LIFE'S AS BAD IN OTHER SCHOOLS AS IT IS IN YOURS? SCHOOLS IN LOADS OF COUNTRIES HAVE THEIR OWN SITES. FIND THEM BY STARTING A SEARCH WITH 'SCHOOLS' OR 'EDUCATION'. TROUBLE IS, MOST OF THEM ARE SET UP BY TEACHERS!

WITH THE INTERNE
TO SEE THE STAR:
SHUTTLE. YOU CA
TO YOUR SCHOOL
THE WORLD. BUT
FREE! THERE'LL B
TO PAY. UNLESS
ARE REALLY GOO
BE LEFT WITHOU

3. THE WEB SITE FOR THE FAMOUS KENNEDY SPACE CENTRE. FIND OUT EVERYTHING ABOUT NASA'S SPACE PROGRAMME, AND EVEN WATCH A SHUTTLE BLAST OFF, LIVE!
(WWW. KSC. nasa. gov/)

4. WATCH A COFFEE PLANT GROW! WHEN THE BEANS ARE RIPE, THEY'RE USED TO MAKE A CUP OF COFFEE. DOES THE SITE THEN BECOME A HAS-BEAN? NO, THE WHOLE THING STARTS AGAIN!
(www. menet. umn. edu/coffeecam/)

SPORTS: 5 STARS: 6 FREE: 7 FRIENDS: 8

5 WEB SITES CARRYING NEWS AND INFORMATION ABOUT MAJOR SPORTING EVENTS ARE VERY POPULAR. THE 1996 OLYMPIC GAMES WEB SITE HAD 189 MILLION VISITORS IN THE 17 DAYS THE GAMES WERE ON, AND 34 MILLION PAGES WERE READ!

6 THERE ARE HUNDREDS OF SITES AROUND DEVOTED TO POP STARS, FILM STARS, SPORTS STARS, AND EVERY OTHER TYPE OF STAR. A SEARCH ON THE NAME OF YOUR FAVORITE IS ABOUT ALL YOU NEED.

(http://www.yahoo.com/entertainment/music/arts/)

OU CAN TRAVEL
ITHOUT A <u>SPACE</u>
END <u>GREETINGS</u>
RIENDS ALL OVER
EWARE - IT'S NOT
ELEPHONE BILLS
OUR PARENTS
ORTS YOU COULD
BEAN!

7 WANT A FREE BASEBALL CAP OR A PACKET OF SEEDS? THERE ARE LOADS OF SITES CRAMMED WITH INFORMATION ABOUT FREE OFFERS ON THE NET. JUST SEARCH `FREEBIES` TO FIND OUT WHERE THEY ARE.

8 POPULAR TV PROGRAMMES LIKE `FRIENDS` ARE BOUND TO HAVE A BATCH OF WEB SITES AND NEWSGROUPS DEVOTED TO THEM. WHAT CAN YOU FIND OUT? FOR A START, OFTEN WHAT HAPPENS NEXT. SOAP FANS IN DIFFERENT COUNTRIES USE THE NET TO TELL EACH OTHER ABOUT EPISODES THEY'VE ALREADY SEEN!

GREETINGS: 1   SCHOOL: 2   SPACE SHUTTLE: 3   BEAN: 4

Nutty newsgroups

Newsgroups are like Internet notice boards. Join a newsgroup and you can send in notices yourself and read what others have written.

There are about 12,000 newsgroups on loads of different subjects. Most are sensible – like the groups which discuss sports and hobbies – but others are totally nutty. You want to read about aliens or cows? Join their newsgroups!

Cheerful chat

The other way Internet users get in touch with each other is through a system called Internet Relay Chat, or IRC for short. That's just a grand name for what amounts to a multi-way conversation. You join a particular "chat-channel" – a TV soap discussion, for instance – and type in what you want to say. Everybody can see what everybody else types, so they can have a good old electronic natter. Sometimes...

In 1997 the VH-1 TV music station organised a live Internet chat with Paul McCartney and asked viewers to send in questions for the 90-minute session. They received over 2 million – enough to keep McCartney chatting for 4 years!

Excellent e-mail

93

Yes, sending an e-mail over the Internet is that quick. No wonder regular users call letters that drop onto your door-mat "snail-mail"!

You can send many copies of the same message to different people just as quickly. They can't say they didn't get it, either. It's often possible to arrange things so that the software sends your note the moment your message is read!

What's more, you're not limited to simply sending words. Anything that can be stored in a computer file can be sent with your e-mail. So not only could your e-mail-pals on the other side of the world get your nifty notes, you could send them pictures, tape recordings and video clips as well!

Crashing fact

To send e-mail to somebody, you need to know their e-mail address. If they have a web site, their e-mail address is often similar. For instance, the address of the President of the United States is
president@whitehouse.gov
Test your English teachers! Ask them if "e-mail" is a real word. If they say no, tell them it's been listed as a verb in Chambers 21st Century Dictionary since 1996.

Keyboard capers
Regular e-mailers make their note-sending even faster by speeding up their typing with *TLA's* and

Smileys...

▶ TLA's are Three-Letter Acronyms (an abbreviation where the first letters of the thing are combined) – like, CUL for "see you later"

▶ Smileys (also known as emoticons) are groups of characters which look like a little picture when viewed sideways on – like the simplest smiley, :-) which means, "I'm feeling happy!"

To read an e-mail packed full of TLA's and smileys takes a bit of know-how. Have you got it? See of you can put this e-mail into English!

BTW a FOAF tells me U R really 8;) HHOJ he sez :-D ISTR U said U R :-[with a :+) and :-)> TTFN!

Answer:

BTW *By the way a* FOAF **friend of a friend** *tells me* U R **you are** *really* 8;) a gorilla. HHOJ Ha-ha, only *joking he sez he says* :-D **laughing out loud.** ISTR I seem to remember U **you** *said* UR **you are** :-[a vampire *with a* :+) **big nose and** :->. a beard.

TTFN! Ta-Ta for now!

Here's a few more for your collection:

TLA'S		SMILEYS	
AFK	AWAY FROM THE KEYBOARD	B-)	I WEAR GLASSES
BFN	BYE FOR NOW	:-~)	I'VE GOT A COLD
GAL	GET A LIFE!	:-@	I'M SCREAMING!
HAND	HAVE A NICE DAY	:-#	I WEAR TEETH BRACES
CBW	IT COULD BE WORSE	I-O	YAWNING
TIC	TONGUE IN CHEEK	:-X	MY LIPS ARE SEALED
TYVM	THANK YOU VERY MUCH	[:-)	I'M WEARING A WALKMAN

What's happening behind the scenes when you log on to the Internet is that you're being allowed to use some of the computers that are connected to it.

There are plenty of other computers linked in that you're *not* allowed to use, though – the computers owned by banks, for instance, and those holding secret information.

And they're the computers that some people just can't resist...

Computer Crookery

Horrible hackers

A "hacker" used to be what a footballer was called if he (or she!) deliberately kicked another player on the shins. Nowadays, it's the name given to somebody who tries to a break into a computer.

Why do they do it? For three reasons:

▶ **Peepers** hack into computers for fun, just to see if they can do it.

▶ **Vandals** set out to cause damage, by changing or even destroying files stored on the computers they hack in to.

▶ **Crooks** hack into a computer for one reason only – to use what they find to make money.

Peepers, vandals or crooks – they're all breaking the law.

Perilous passwords

So, you'd like to know how a hacker breaks into a computer? Tough! You're not going to find out here!

What most people know, though, is that most computers on a network will at least ask for a name and a password before you're allowed any further. So the first thing a hacker has to do is to discover a real name and a password to go with it.

The name is usually the easy bit. Hackers often know the name of somebody who uses the computer and, if they don't, trying "Smith", "Brown" or other common names will be an obvious place to start.

Guessing a password is a lot tougher. (Don't believe the films where the hero can do it in a couple of tries!). At least, it should be a lot tougher. When it isn't, it's usually because the password is one that's easy to guess.

So, what's a rotten password? Try this simple test. Which out of the following wouldn't be a good idea for password? And which would be the worst?

1 The name of your husband or wife (or best friend if you're not old enough to have a husband or wife!).

2 Your favourite sports team.

3 Your favourite pop star or sports person.

4 A very rude word.

Answer: They'd all be bad, because the number of different possibilities is quite small, making them easier to guess – especially if the hacker knows you. But worst of all is the rude word! In a 1997 survey carried out by the computer manufacturer Compaq, over 30% of computer users had a rude word for their password!

Get me the Pentagon!

Of all the hacking targets in the world, the most attractive seems to be the USA's defence HQ, The Pentagon. In 1997 it was subject to 250,000 attacks!

How many of these attacks were successful isn't known. It's claimed that all the Pentagon's computer cables run through special tubes designed to show up any unauthorized connection.

Special or not, they didn't stop one German hacker. His name was Markus Hess, and this is what he managed to do over a period of two years starting in 1986...

▶ Using a PC from his flat in Hanover, he discovered some passwords which let him connect to a computer at Hanover University.

▶ From there, he was able to link to the European Academic Research Network, a collection of computers at other German universities. By searching around this network he managed to break into a computer at Bremen University.

▶ The computer at Bremen had a special link to the USA. Hess used it to connect his PC to the United States University Research Network. It wasn't long before he'd managed to hack into a computer at Lawrence Berkeley Laboratories, over 6,000 miles away in California!

▶ Lawrence Berkeley was an important laboratory, doing a lot of research work for the US Armed Forces. A few more passwords broken, and Hess found himself connected to the US Military Network!

▶ Pretending to be a soldier named "Colonel

Albrens", code name "Hunter", Hess carried on his hacking.

▶ He got into 30 top-secret American defence computers and read top-secret Pentagon files.

▶ He even managed to read and copy documents about spy satellites and nuclear warfare before he was caught.

MARKUS LIKES TO GET INTO CHARACTER WHEN HE'S HACKING

And how was he caught? By using computer time worth less than a dollar!

Anybody allowed to work on the computers at Lawrence Berkeley Laboratory still had to pay for the computer time they used. Hess, of course, wasn't allowed! So when Cliff Stoll, the computer manager at the laboratory, was checking the accounts he discovered that the figures didn't add up – they were 75 cents (about 50p) out!

Most people would have ignored such a pathetic amount, but Stoll didn't. He wanted to know why his sums weren't right. So he began exploring ... and came to the conclusion that it could only have been caused by a hacker using time on the computer.

So Stoll began a one-man hunt, spying on the Hess the spy – until the hacker was finally tracked down and arrested. (If you want to read the fully story it's in Clifford Stoll's book, *The Cuckoo's Egg*.)

Vicious viruses

What have these two got in common?

Answer: They've both got a virus!

Just like we can catch cold and 'flu viruses that make us feel rotten, computers can "catch" viruses which do nasty things when they're run. The difference is that while nobody gives us their cold on purpose, computer viruses – programs which hide and reproduce themselves – are spread deliberately.

The picture in the computer screen shows one of

the most famous viruses at work. Called the "Christmas tree" virus, it suddenly started appearing on computer screens of the company IBM in 1987.

Along with the picture came the message -
"Let this run and enjoy yourself. Just type Christmas."

What happened when users did type it? They unknowingly sent the virus off to another IBM computer. Within hours the virus had spread as far as IBM offices in Germany, Italy and Japan!

That virus gummed up the works of IBM's computers for a few hours, but apart from that it didn't do anything nasty. Other viruses have been a lot more vicious. In 1988 a "time bomb" virus sent to the Jerusalem University computer was found not a moment too soon. Planted by an anti-Jewish vandal, it was set to wreck all the computer's files on 13 May – the 40th anniversary of the birth of modern Israel.

Computer crooks (CR, WC)

Once upon a time crooks pulled out guns and tried to rob banks. Nowadays, with money being sent around the world over computer networks, crooks work in a different way – they pull out *keyboards* and try to rob banks!

Fortunately, crashing computers are often matched by crashing crooks! Like these...

▶ In 1992, an American computer operator in charge of printing his company's salary cheques saw a way of making himself some extra money. He waited until his own name came up – and then got the computer to print not one salary cheque for him but 30 of them! How was he caught? The idiot tried to pay them all into his bank at the same time!

▶ In 1986 a 14-year-old boy in Auckland, New Zealand, could have carried out a fantastic heist – if he hadn't lost his nerve. Putting an envelope into one of his bank's machines, he keyed in that he'd just deposited $1 million NZ dollars. In fact he hadn't. The only thing the envelope had in it was a lump of card from a lollipop packet!

It had been done as a joke but, to his amazement, when the boy checked his bank account a couple of days later it said the $1 million was there!

So he took $10 out as a test. It worked! Next day he took out $500 – and that worked too!

And the day after that? That's when his nerve failed. He put the $500 back again and admitted what he'd done.

(Just as well. He would have been found out in the end. The bank had just been very slow in comparing the money they actually received against the money recorded by their computer.)

In the world of high technology, though, you don't have rob a computerized bank to make a fortune. There are other ways...

▶ In 1990, a Californian named Kevin Poulson hacked his way into a radio station's telephone system and computers to give himself an advantage with their phone-in competitions. But he didn't know when to stop – and police became suspicious after he'd won 2 Porsches, 2 trips to Hawaii and $20,000 in cash! He was arrested and charged with computer espionage.

That's the trouble with crooks. They get greedy, and it catches them out in the end...

▶ In 1996 an Irish boy ordered thousands of pounds worth of chocolate over the Internet by typing in a credit card number at random. Although the number was accepted – and a bill went to its owner (in Argentina!) – police managed to track the boy down. What's more, they arrived before he'd eaten all evidence. Did he feel sick!

Crashing fact
Internet users, often not knowing it's against the law, steal music regularly! How? By copying tracks which are illegally put onto the network. In 1998, one album by the group Oasis was on the Internet $1^1/_2$ wks before it reached the shops!

Computerised crime fighters!
Crooks may be using computers nowadays, but the police are too. So tell your teachers that if they're fed up with being badly paid teachers and have decided to become well-paid crooks here are a few good reasons to make them think again!

Lennie Leggitt, the world's most convicted shoplifter, stood up and gripped the rails of the dock. He looked glumly across at the red-robed judge and sighed miserably. It had happened again.

"Leonard Leggitt," said the judge, "you have been found guilty of all charges. Before I pass sentence, have you anything to say?"

"Yeah, I have," yelled Lennie. "It ain't fair! Using computers against a crook who's only trying to do an honest day's thieving. It's ... it's..."

"Daylight robbery?"

"Near enough," Lennie moaned. "I mean, take that jewellery shop. The one I where I went to pick up a necklace for my dear wife."

"Pick up without paying for," corrected the judge.

"Yeah, all right. But that security camera was real!"

"Really?"

"Talk about sneaky. Some shops save money by sticking up cameras which ain't real. They're dummies. Until now, any self-respecting villain could tell the difference between a real one and a dummy. But what did they do? Put up a real one wot looked like a dummy!"

The judge smiled. "A camera which caught you in the act and made you look like a dummy!"

"Right. Then, when I legged it, what do I find? While  I've been away, me getaway car's been checked out by a traffic warden carryin' a computer in her pocket. She's used it to send me number to some central computer – and found out I've got a couple of unpaid parking tickets."

"A couple of hundred unpaid parking tickets," corrected the judge again.

"All right. So what have they done? Towed me car off!"

"What you might called the getaway car that got away!"

"Well, I didn't have any choice then, did I? I had to

107

nick one. Nice red job, it was, one of my favourites. In
I get ... only to find I've been fooled by another
computer!"

A jolly laugh came from Lennie's side. "Our computer,"
chuckled PC Lock, the burly policeman guarding him in
the dock. "One of our lads has checked through all the
data on stolen cars and come up with the fact that nice
red jobs are most likely to get pinched..."

"So what do they do?" said Lennie. "They get a red
car, put in a likely place, and wait for somebody to come
along. I end up nicking a police car!"

"And they end up nicking you!"
said the judge cheerfully. "Stealing
cars and stealing jewellery."

Lennie moaned. "It ain't fair. I'd
dumped the necklace. Thought I
could say it was somebody else on
the security camera. I mean, those things make you look
right ugly."

"You are right ugly."

"I mean they make everybody look right ugly. I was
going to claim it was somebody else. Say I'd never been
near the place." Lennie shook his head and sighed. "No
good. Computers got me again."

PC Lock wagged his finger under Lennie's nose.
"Teach you to take your mobile phone on a job, won't
it?"

"I only had it give my Mavis a ring
when I was on me way home."

"A ring about the necklace," chuckled
PC Lock. "Very good, Lennie."

"How was I to know mobile phones send a non-stop
signal telling the phone company's computer

whereabouts it is? And stores it all for two years!"

"In other words, the computer stored the store you'd been to!" laughed the judge. He wiped his eyes, then looked down at the unhappy crook. "Good things, computers. Wouldn't you say?"

Lennie nodded. "I'm convinced."

"Which will make you a convinced convict! I sentence you to three years in jail. And by the time you come out I hope you'll be a wiser man!"

"I will, yer honour. I'm going to spend the time studying."

"Studying? Excellent! What subject?"

"Computers! I want to know what I'll be up against when I get out!"

Crashing fact

Judges in Scotland have started using portable computers which hold details of 6,000 crimes and sentences. To help them pass an appropriate sentence they simply have to look up: "jewel robbery" or "car theft" to find out what sentence criminals have been given in the past. In other words, some crooks are not only caught by computer – they meet a computer in court!

But if you want to find the crookedest crooks and the nastiest villains, there's really only one place to go. Into the world of computer games...

Games Galore

Computer games have been around almost as long as computers – and that's a fact.

In 1860 Charles Babbage designed (but – surprise, surprise! – didn't finish) a machine to play noughts-and-crosses. His idea was to put six of them in a room and charge children to use them – another example of Babbage not being quite so barmy after all. Without knowing it, he'd dreamt up the idea of the arcade game over 100 years before it arrived...

Computer games timeline

1972 "Pong" appears in a bar in Seattle, USA. It's made by a company named Atari and is nothing to do with smells. It's an electronic version of tennis in which two players use their "bats" (a small oblong on the screen which they move with a joystick) to hit a "ball" (a white blob) across the "net" (a line down the middle of the screen). In spite of being in black-and-white and lasting only three minutes, Pong is a smash hit! (Well, it was a *tennis* game!)

1978 The first shoot 'em up game, *Space Invaders*, takes

110

over as the top game in pubs and clubs. People find the challenge of picking off ranks of spider-shaped aliens so addictive that an MP tries to have the game banned!

1980 Atari, Commodore and other USA-based companies launch games for home use. You can either buy them as cartridges to play on a special games machine, or on disks for a home computer. They sell like crazy, until...

1983 Home computers start to be used for serious things, and games go out of fashion! From being worth $3 billion a year, the American games market collapses to a fraction of that size in twelve months.

1985 It takes a Japanese company, Nintendo, to revive things with a hand-held device called a "Game-Boy". It comes with a screen-clearing game called *Tetris*, which goes on to sell 40 million copies!

1986 The same company follow up with their Nintendo Entertainment

System. It's the first real games console, and comes with the first game to feature a star character as its hero. His name's Mario. Is he dashing? No. He's a dumpy Italian plumber!

1989 PC games begin to appear on CD-ROMs, giving them the capability to include more complicated screen displays and sound effects. The only problem is that PC's with CD-ROM drives cost a fortune!

1991 Another big Japanese company, Sega, launches its console with a game featuring another curious leading character. His name's Sonic and he's a blue, jumping, spinning hedgehog.

1994 A third Japanese company, Sony, join the market with their PlayStation consoles. The big three of Nintendo, Sony and Sega have dominated the games console market ever since.

1997 Nintendo introduce their N64 console. It's the fastest games console ever.

1998 Games freaks who couldn't bear to be parted from their 1980's Atari games cash in; the £5 games now sell to collectors for £500!

2000, 2001, 2002...
Predictions! The best-selling computer gaming accessory for the next few Christmases will be the same as for the past few: batteries! Over 4 billion are sold annually, 40% of them around Christmas

ARE THEY GOING TO A GOOD HOME?

OH, GOODY, MORE BATTERIES

Gruesome games quiz

Grown-ups often complain that many computer games are just shoot-'em-up or knock-'em-down affairs full of blood and thunder – which they are, of course!

What they don't realize is that modern computer games are a bit like books. They may sometimes be telling a gruesome story, but they usually have heroes and villains – and it's the player's job to see that the hero wins the day.

So prepare yourself for the next time your parents complain by trying this quick quiz. Can you prove you know whose side you should be on by sorting out the heroes from the villains?

1 "Bomberman" appears in the game of the same name. He journeys around a maze and – guess what? – bombs things. **Hero or villain?**

2 "Consumer" is a purple-haired cannibal whose sharpened teeth are capable of cutting through bone in a single bite. **Hero or villain?**

3 An enormous training shoe. **Hero or villain?**

4 A vampire who fatally wounds enemies in battle and then finishes them off by drinking their blood. **Hero or villain?**

114

5 A endless supply of armadillos. **Heroes or villains?**

6 A frog-dinosaur. **Hero or villain?**

7 A character who sneers, "wanna run home to mama now?". **Hero or villain?**

8 Bloaty Head. **Hero or villain?**

against predators. Leaping, squashing frog-dinosaurs are a powerful weapon!

7 Hero. It's one of the taunts made by the player of the *Virtual Fighter* games whenever an enemy is shot down.

8 Villain – but Bloaty Head is a disease, not a person. It features in a game called *Theme Hospital* in which you have to make money by running a hospital and curing patients who turn up suffering from odd diseases.

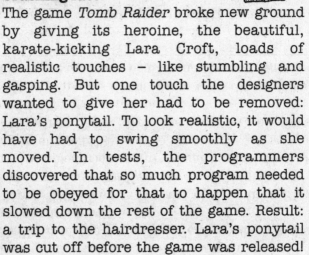

Crashing fact

The game *Tomb Raider* broke new ground by giving its heroine, the beautiful, karate-kicking Lara Croft, loads of realistic touches – like stumbling and gasping. But one touch the designers wanted to give her had to be removed: Lara's ponytail. To look realistic, it would have had to swing smoothly as she moved. In tests, the programmers discovered that so much program needed to be obeyed for that to happen that it slowed down the rest of the game. Result: a trip to the hairdresser. Lara's ponytail was cut off before the game was released!

Tales of the unexpected: random numbers

You've got a new game. It's called *Skinhead!* and its

hero is a long-haired guy called Super Hairio. The object of the game is to get Hairio from home to work without being caught by demon barbers who leap out and try to cut his hair. (Admit it – the game sounds "shear" magic!)

The demon barbers are typical baddies. All computer games have them, and the challenge is to dodge them or deal with them. To make that more difficult, they pop up at odd times and in odd places. If they didn't – if, for instance, demon barber Number One always raced out of the first door on the right exactly two seconds after the game started – then the game wouldn't be such a challenge. So, how do the baddies in computer games change their tactics?

It's all done by random numbers – that is, values you can't predict. (A bit like the answers to your maths homework!)

Here's an example. Say you're the games programmer and want barber Number One to jump out somewhere between 0 and 6 seconds after the game begins. What you could do is some simple (honestly!) arithmetic. Like this:

- ▶ pick any number you like – say, 345
- ▶ divide 345 by 7 – giving the answer 49 and remainder 2
- ▶ use the remainder ... and make barber Number One jump out after 2 seconds!

(If you divide the screen display into different areas, then exactly the same method could be used to decide which area the barber appears from).

How about the next demon barber? Just use the same method again. We don't want barbers turning up every 2 seconds, though, so first you'll have to find another number...

- ▶ from the first sum, put the remainder in front of the answer. That is, put 2 in front of 49 to give your next number – 249
- ▶ divide 249 by 7 – giving the answer 35 and remainder 4
- ▶ use the remainder – barber Number Two jumps out 4 seconds after barber Number One!

And so it goes on, with Super Hairio feeling more and more cut up about things as the barbers appear at random times.

There's a problem, though. How does the opening number (345 in the example) change every time the game is played? Simple. The game either has a stack of numbers which it uses (at random, of course), or else it finds a new start number when the game's first entered – such as the time of day.

Get up at a quarter-past six to play *Skinhead!* and the start number could be 615; stay up late and the start number might be 1129.

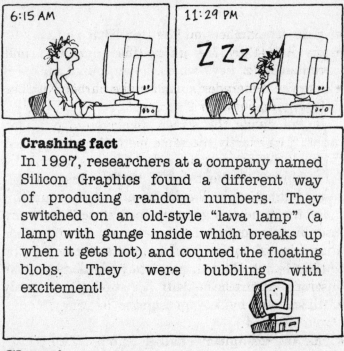

Crashing fact

In 1997, researchers at a company named Silicon Graphics found a different way of producing random numbers. They switched on an old-style "lava lamp" (a lamp with gunge inside which breaks up when it gets hot) and counted the floating blobs. They were bubbling with excitement!

Cheat!

It happens every time. A few months after a game comes out, somebody will come along and tell you how to cheat at it. The "cheat" may gain you extra lives and allow you to skip levels – lots of different cheats exist. But why? Are they examples of crashing computers?

No, they're actually the opposite. Like any computer program, before a game goes on sale it has to be tested to make sure it works properly. Now, put yourself in the position of the game tester. You play the game all the way through to level 99 – and then you find an error. Having changed the program, you really wouldn't want to play it all the way through again to make sure your change works – you'd want to skip straight to that part. So what you do is to write into the program a check for a curious combination of keys which, when found, makes it skip levels 1 – 98 and jump straight to level 99!

By the time the game is fully tested there are usually so many of these secret key combinations that it's too much trouble taking them out. So they're left in the game, but not mentioned in the instructions that come with it – staying secret only until somebody discovers them!

Crashing computer cheats

Even Tamagotchi pets have cheats built into them. Attracted by a competition to find the oldest surviving Tamagotchi, some owners discovered that by pressing buttons in unexpected sequences it was possible to make their pet older than it really was. Competition judges had no trouble spotting their entries, though – they were the ones claiming their pets had lived longer than they'd been on sale!

Is that all you've got to do?

Is playing computer games good for you, or bad for you? Easy! You think they're good, your parents and teachers think they're bad – and it's not just because they can't play them as well as you either. Many adults think computer games are a waste of time. So, if you've got somebody like that at home, learn this quotation off by heart:

"The British Educational Communications and Technology Agency (BECTA) has recognised that games can help players:
▶ **learn to think quickly**
▶ **improve their attention span**
▶ **learn from experience**
▶ **become familiar with new technology"**

(They're also great fun, but you don't have to mention that if you don't want to!)

Of course, parents and teachers won't take that lying down. They'll come back with arguments to show that playing computer games is bad – so you've got to know how to handle them.

For instance, they might try saying something like: "if you keep on playing computer games, you'll end up suffering from…"

From what? Try this ailment test. Which of the complaints in this list has it been shown that computer games players can suffer from?

a Repetitive strain injuries (called RSI, especially sore wrists and fingers).

b Pains in the neck (real pains, not nagging parents and teachers!).

c Tendinitis, tenosynovitis and carpal tunnel

syndrome (inflammations of the tendons leading to your fingers).

d Peripheral neuropathy (like your hands still shaking and twitching after you've left the keyboard).

e Enuresis and encoprisis (wanting to go to the loo when you're asleep – and not waking up in time!).

f Epileptic seizures (feeling faint, maybe even losing consciousness).

Answer:

Gulp ... all of them! Games players *can* suffer from the lot – but almost always because they've been playing for far too long in the wrong conditions. What you'll have to say is that you always (well, you will in the future anyway)...

▶ play in a well-lit room

▶ play for short periods at a time, not hours on end

▶ sit the full distance possible from screen

▶ stop at once if you feel unwell

Crashing fact

Computer games can also damage your football, according to David James, the Liverpool goalkeeper. In 1997, shortly after being given a Sony PlayStation, he had an awful match – and promptly blamed his poor performance on the fact that he was half asleep. He'd stayed up too late playing games the night before!

A computer? Really?

When is a computer game not a computer game? When it's for real...

Pilot to ground control!

You strap herself into the pilot's seat with a giggle. Fancy! Little old you, allowed to fly a big aeroplane like this! What did they call it? A Boeing 747. You'll have to remember that for when you get home. If you get home...

You peep out through the front screen. The runway stretches off into the distance, a line of bright lights showing the way. Good job, too. You hadn't even realized it was getting dark!

Turning your head to one side, you see the outline of the airport buildings. Looking the other way, you see a fire engine standing by. And an ambulance. Charming! Don't they believe you can fly this plane?

It's time to go! You bring the plane's engines to full throttle, then send the 747 hurtling down the runway. You see the lights flashing beneath the body of the plane and hear the wind whistling over its wings.

At exactly the right moment, you ease back the controls – and bring the huge plane off the ground!

You flick a switch, and hear the comforting clunk of the plane's wheels coming up.

Glancing out of the cockpit windows again you find that the airport buildings are already way beneath you. Ahead you can see the deepening red of the sky where the sun is dipping below the distant horizon amid streaks of grey cloud.

And what else can you see? Oh, yes, there's a small aeroplane flying across in front of you...

What?!! What's that doing there? You're going to hit it!

Come on, you've got to do something fast! But what?

Dive? You'll hit the ground!
Swerve? You'll hit the plane!
Go higher? Maybe...

You've got a split second to make up your mind!

Too late. You've had it.

With a horrible crunch you plough straight into the other plane. Everything goes black. Are you dead? For an instant you think you might be – until you hear a voice crackle through your headphones.

"You blew it! Game over!"

That's an example of what it's like to be playing a *virtual reality* (VR) game. Instead of watching a screen and using a keyboard or gamepad to control a character, a VR game puts you in the middle of the action!

All you need, as well as a powerful computer and specially written software, is:

I FEEL A VIRTUAL IDIOT IN THIS LOT!

▶ a **VR headset** – a kind of Darth Vader helmet which has a wraparound screen at the front so that the view changes as you look around. It will have twin speakers to give you sound effects as well.

▶ a **VR glove** – a glove that detects when you're moving your fingers, and sends back sensations. A very handy device, in fact!

With these on, outside noises and sensations disappear and your brain is fooled. You're in a virtual world – a world that doesn't exist, but feels as if it does!

Can you be fooled?

Think you've got a brain that can't be fooled? Then try this little quiz about some VR experiences and see if you're right!

1 You can see the rolling waves. If you're not careful, they'll come crashing down on top of you. As the sea races beneath you, you're having trouble keeping your balance. What are you doing?

    a Riding a VR surfboard.

    b Sailing a VR yacht.

    c Being towed on VR water-skis.

2 You are not alone, but one of a team. You're in a cramped space. There are lots of other teams around you, doing the same thing. Some of the them are friendly – but others are trying to knock you out! What are you doing?

    a VR wrestling, as one of a VR tag team.

    b Pretending to be a VR medicine battling against VR germs.

    c Fighting a VR battle in a VR tank.

3 You're struggling with all your might. The computer-controlled object in your hands feels as though it's going to break! What are you doing?

    a Knocking down a VR wall with a VR sledge-hammer.

    b VR deep-sea fishing.

    c Trying to break a VR alien's neck during a VR invasion.

4 You're tootling happily along. Suddenly something comes at you from the side and crashes into you! What's happened?

   a You've been tackled in a VR rugby match.

   b You've had a VR car crash.

   c You've been hit by a VR trolley at a VR supermarket.

5 You're sitting at a real desk in a real room with plain-coloured (but real) walls. Where are you?

   a In a VR TV studio.

   b In a VR classroom.

   c In a VR office.

6 You're on a theme park ride in the year 2002 – and it's the slowest ride you've ever been on! It doesn't swerve, dive, plummet or do anything exciting. It just crawls along. Where's the ride supposed to be taking you?

   a On a VR trip to the bottom of the ocean.

   b On a VR voyage through your stomach.

   c On a VR journey across the moon.

Answers:

1 – a Surfers (of waves, not the Net) can practise in the lounge by riding a virtual surfboard! It stands on legs which move it up and down. A VR headset shows you the rolling sea as you try to keep your balance (and stop yourself being seasick!).

2 – c It's a system tank crews use for training. What's more, it is networked, so they can have pretend battles against tank crews in other countries. Maybe that's the way to fight wars in future.

3 – b It's a VR system with a computer-controlled fishing rod that bends just as it would if a real-life fish was struggling on the end of their line!

4 – b The car manufacturer Volvo have developed a VR system to show what it's like to be inside a car that's hit by another travelling at just 25 miles per hour. Now that's what you call a crashing computer!

5 – a Many TV programs, such as the news bulletins or BBC's *Match of the Day*, are broadcast from a "virtual studio". The viewer thinks the presenters are in a studio full of snazzy backgrounds, but it's not true. They're actually in front of a plain-coloured screen displaying *pictures* of snazzy backgrounds. It's a system that can easily crash, though. If the presenter wears anything that's the same colour as the screen ... it disappears!

6 – c An American company, Lunacorp, want to launch a rocket to the moon and land a robot car which will trundle round, beaming back pictures to a VR moon buggy ride at a space travel theme park. You'll have to wait a while for a go on it, though. 2001 is when the company "plan-it" will be ready!

Crashing fact
VR headsets could soon smell horrible ... or delicious. Developers are working on different pongs to go with VR trips. One company in the USA has even produced a VR tour through Willie Wonka's Chocolate Factory – complete with chocolate and marshmallow smells!

Riotous Robots

How do you tell the difference between a teacher and a computer? Here are some tell-tale signs:

▶ Computers have odd, droning voices; teachers ... er, forget that one.

▶ Some computers are on a trolley; some teachers are off their trolley ... No, forget that one too.

▶ Teachers have dodgy hairstyles and trousers that don't fit properly (and the men are just as bad); computers don't...

Hang on, let's start again.

▶ Teachers have eyes in the front of their heads (and some have them in the backs of their heads as well); computers don't.

▶ Teachers have ears that can pick up the softest whisper; computers don't.

▶ Teachers have noses that can smell trouble; computers don't.

▶ Teachers can point the way to the headteacher's study – and walk there with you if necessary; computers can't.

But what if a computer did have some or all these abilities? What if it could see and hear and move about? Would it be a teacher? No – it would be a robot!

> **Crashing fact**
> "Robot" is a Czechoslovakian word meaning "forced labour". It was first used in a 1921 play by the author Karel Capek as a name for mechanical workers.

I will obey!

A robot is a computer-controlled machine with "human-like" qualities:

EARS:
(MICROPHONES)
THROUGH WHICH
THE COMPUTER
CAN INPUT NOISE

EYES:
(CAMERAS)
THROUGH WHICH
THE COMPUTER
CAN INPUT
PICTURES

MOUTH:
(LOUDSPEAKER)
THROUGH WHICH
THE COMPUTER
CAN OUTPUT
SOUND

LEGS:
(SOMETIMES
METAL RODS
LIKE THE
ARMS. BUT
OFTEN JUST A
SET OF WHEELS)
WHICH THE
COMPUTER CAN
DIRECT AND MOVE

ARMS AND HANDS:
(OFTEN GAS-POWERED
METAL RODS WITH
CLAWS ON THE END)
WHICH THE COMPUTER
CAN POSITION AND
USE TO MANIPULATE
THINGS

But how does a robot act in a human-like way? How easily can it be programmed to do jobs that humans do? Important jobs like – being a dinner lady...

WITH ITS MICROPHONE EARS A ROBOT CAN PICK UP SOUNDS. BUT THAT'S NOT ENOUGH. THE COMPUTER MUST BE PROGRAMMED TO TELL ONE SOUND FROM ANOTHER...

FOR A ROBOT TO MOVE ANYWHERE ITS COMPUTER HAS TO DECIDE WHICH DIRECTION IT HAS TO GO IN, THEN SEND THE NECESSARY INSTRUCTIONS TELLING ITS "LEGS" TO TURN RIGHT, TURN LEFT, GO FORWARD AND SO ON. THIS ALSO MEANS IT MUST HAVE AN ACCURATE MAP STORED IN ITS MEMORY...

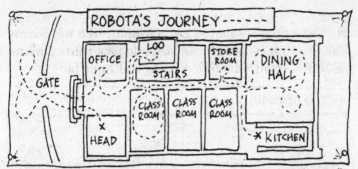

ON THE JOURNEY A GOOD ROBOT WILL USE ITS "EYES" TO STOP IF SOMETHING GETS IN ITS WAY...

DOING SOMETHING USEFUL IS THE HARDEST JOB OF ALL. THE COMPUTER NEEDS TO HAVE A CLEAR "PICTURE" IN ITS MEMORY OF WHAT IT WILL BE WORKING WITH...

IT THEN HAS TO RECOGNIZE WHAT IT'S LOOKING FOR IN THE REAL WORLD. THIS ISN'T AS EASY AS IT SOUNDS. PICTURES ARE MURDER FOR A COMPUTER TO RECOGNIZE BECAUSE THEY ARE INPUT AS A PATTERN OF DOTS. ALL IT CAN DO IS TRY TO JUGGLE THE PATTERN IT'S RECEIVED AND TRY TO MATCH IT AGAINST THE PATTERN IN ITS MEMORY...

ONLY THEN CAN THE COMPUTER ISSUE THE COMMANDS TO THE ROBOT'S ARMS TO PICK UP WHAT IT'S FOUND. THIS TOO, IS REALLY TRICKY. TO PICK SOMETHING UP, THE ROBOT'S FINGERS MUST CLOSE ON IT BY JUST THE RIGHT AMOUNT. IF IT DOESN'T GRIP TIGHTLY ENOUGH, YOU'VE GOT PROBLEMS...

BUT IF THE ROBOT GRIPS TOO TIGHTLY, MORE PROBLEMS...

FINALLY, THE OBJECT HAS TO BE PLACED ACCURATELY IN POSITION — ANOTHER TEST OF HOW WELL THE COMPUTER CAN MAP WHAT IT "SEES" AGAINST THE MAP IN ITS MEMORY...

Don't get the idea that Robota is a typical robot. She isn't. Throughout the world there are at least one million robots working away without a problem. Many of these are making cars – a job that's a lot easier than being a dinner-lady!

These robots are called "immobots", because they're immobile. That is, the robots stay in one place and the work comes to them – like a bare car arriving in front of a paint-spraying robot, for instance. The robot then paints it by following the same path every time.

There's one vitally important condition, though. Prove it for yourself with this experiment.

▶ Unwrap a toffee, put it in your right hand and hold your right arm straight out in front of you.

▶ Ask a toffee-loving ~~idiot~~ friend to stand so that their open mouth is right in front of your hand.

▶ Pop the toffee in their mouth, then send your ~~idiot~~ friend away.

▶ Put your arm down, and unwrap another toffee

▶ Call your ~~idiot~~ friend back and ask him to stand in exactly the same place as before

▶ Now raise your arm again and pop in the next toffee. If it goes up their nose or in their eye or anywhere other than their mouth then you've proved the important condition!

WHY WOULD ANYONE WANT A ROBOT FOR STICKING TOFFEES UP THEIR NOSE?

SHUT UP! IT'S AN EXPERIMENT

Robots like these follow their programmed pattern of movements come what may. If what they're supposed to be working on hasn't been positioned properly, too bad. They'll just carry regardless – so that the car ends up half sprayed, or, worse, behaves like an automatic tunnel-digging robot that was set up to dig up a street in Seattle, USA, in 1996. In this case it was the street that hadn't been positioned properly – so that when the robot began to follow the route it had been given, it disappeared underground! Not only did it end up digging a 200-metre hole in the wrong place ... it cost $600,000 to fill up again. (Which must have put a hole in their budget!)

Reliable robots

Robot design is getting a lot more reliable, though. Just as well. Let's hope none of these ever get out of control...

▶ The Japanese company Honda have invented a human-like robot to wheel trolleys around a factory. They claim that its sensors are so clever that it can't possibly lose it's way or bump into people. Let's hope not. The robot is 2 metres tall and weighs 210 Kg! (33 stone)

▶ Robots don't have to be huge, though – especially if they've been designed to take trips through our bodies! In 1998 a French surgeon used micro-robot cameras and surgical tools to carry out six heart operations. Controlling them with the aid of a special screen, he was able to operate

on diseased parts of the heart that can't normally be reached.

▶ Is your school heating always going wrong? Maybe you need Monika! Designed in Denmark, Monika is a robo-doll who can be heated up and used to test what's causing offices (or class-rooms) to become too cold.

▶ Ever wondered how deep sea oil-rigs have their legs checked for rustiness? Until now it's been a job for humans, but a diving robot will soon be changing all that. Not only can it stay under the freezing water for far longer than human divers, it doesn't need to have a constant supply of hot air or water pumped round its diving suit to keep it warm! Does that make it a hot-bot?

▶ Tiny robot soldiers are expected to be marching by 2001. A project in the USA aims to develop shoebox-sized robots to crawl, hop and fly around doing jobs like clearing land mines, detecting chemical weapons and any other dangerous job the human troops don't fancy.

▶ Various robot competitions have been held, from maze-searching to table-tennis to a football-playing tournament as part of the World Cup '98 celebrations in France. But the oddest of all must the robot street performer contest held in Tokyo in 1997. The list of competitors included:

▶ a cane-swinging robot which danced like Charlie Chaplin and tripped over a carpet.

▶ A smoking robot.

▶ A mechanical frog robot that blew bubbles and croaked.

▶ And the winner, a robot monkey who played the xylophone!

▶ Finally – the most famous doll in the world has been turned into a robot! There is now a version of "Barbie" that can be linked to a PC and programmed with answers to questions. Of course, Barbie's slim figure has to be maintained at all costs. So the necessary electronic circuitry is packed in her stomach and the batteries are hidden in her legs!

Crashing fact

A robot was arrested in 1982, loitering with intent in Beverley Hills, USA. It was a radio-controlled robot being operated by two teenagers who'd borrowed it from their Dad's company – and, when the police arrived, were nowhere to be seen. So the lawmen tried to take the robot to bits to find out where it had come from. As they did the robot yelped, "Help me! They're trying to take me apart!"

I am thick ... I think!

The reason robots have so much trouble with jobs that humans find incredibly simple (like recognising a hot-dog from different angles) is that a robot's "brain" is a computer while humans have real brains!

Computers may be fast and able to remember a lot, but they're only able to follow the instructions they've been given to obey. But will it ever be possible to program them with "artificial intelligence" – that is, give them the ability to think like humans?

That's a question the inventor of the Colossus

computer, Alan Turing, asked in 1950. He suggested that a good way to prove it would be with an "artificial intelligence" test which has become known as the Turing Test...

▶ Without knowing which is which, an interrogator asks questions of two "people" – one a human, and the other a computer.

▶ From the answers (which can be lies) the interrogator has to work out which is the computer and which is the human.

▶ If the interrogator gets it wrong, then the computer has shown itself to be "intelligent"!

So far, no computer has passed this test. Why not? Because computers store and use information, but they don't *understand* it...

Checkmate, mate!
In 1997, an IBM chess-playing computer, Deep Blue, caused a sensation when it beat the world champion Gary Kasparov. Did this prove that Deep Blue was as intelligent as Kasparov?

No. It proved that the computer was fast enough to test out thousands of possible moves before it chose the one it was going to make. Even that wasn't enough in the first couple of games which Kasparov won.

What made the difference was that Deep Blue's

programmers brought in a secret weapon – another human chess champion to check the computer's moves to see if they were any good!

Compainters and compoets

Computers have been programmed to paint, and write poetry and short stories. Does this make them intelligent?

No. It's done by writing programs that have the computers choose colours or rhyming patterns or story phrases from the vast number that they've had keyed into their memory. The computer doesn't have a clue whether they're good or not.

And sometimes they *are* good! Paintings produced by a computer named Aaron at the University of California sell for $2,000 a time! But does Aaron understand what "he" is doing? Of course not – otherwise why would he let his programmer keep all the money!

Besides, for every expert who likes Aaron's paintings there's another who reckons they're – well, the sort that this poem's talking about (a poem that *wasn't* written by a computer):

> Anyone can make mistakes
>   That fact is true indeed,
> But to really mess things up
> A computer's what you need!

Very funny

You'll be delighted to know that a real test of intelligence is telling jokes. (Make sure your teacher appreciates this when you're caught behind the bike sheds telling a naughty one!) Here's a computer quip from Jape-1, a joke-telling computer.

So is Jape-1 intelligent? No. It's just a computer using a dictionary of words and phrases, together with facts about how they're pronunced. To invent its joke, Jape would have:

▶ found the phrase "fur coat"
▶ looked at its definition, "something to wear"
▶ found "fir", as a word that sounded the same as "fur"
▶ looked at its definition, "a tree"
▶ then mixed the two definitions and words together.

Jape-1 could just have easily invented the joke: "What kind of coat grows to 30m? A fir coat!"

Now compare this with a human joke:

You may have groaned, but did you understand that joke? Of course you did – which just shows how intelligent you are! Because you needed to know –

▶ that the phrase "my heart isn't in it" is another way of saying that you're not enjoying yourself.

▶ that a living person is made of bones and other important bits, like a heart.

▶ that the bone collection is called a skeleton.

▶ that when a person has been dead for a while, all that's left is the skeleton – that is, an article whose heart isn't in it!

Crashing fiction

One of the most intelligent, and certainly the most famous, fictional computers was HAL 9000, the computer star of the film *2001: A Space Odyssey*. HAL is in charge of a mission so secret that not even the human crew are allowed to know what it is. When they try to find out, intelligent HAL decides to kill them!

The plan backfires, though. One of the crew survives and comes up with an even smarter solution – kill HAL. That's humans for you: dead clever!

Please computer!

But what if computers could be given real intelligence? So much intelligence that they became as brainy as the brainiest brains in brainy-land. That is ... as clever as a teacher!

Would a computer do their job better?

145

I CAN CONNECT YOU TO THE WORLD AS WELL, SCROGGINS. I COULD HELP YOU CONTACT OTHER YOUNGSTERS ALL OVER THE GLOBE. ALL CANADIAN PUPILS HAVE THEIR OWN E-MAIL ADDRESSES, YOU KNOW. AND THEN THERE'S THE INTERNET OF COURSE...

THE INTERNET! BRILLIANT!

THE INTERNET, NOW THERE'S A THOUGHT! DID I TELL YOU ABOUT THE NURSERY SCHOOL IN AMERICA, SCROGGINS? THE ONE THAT HAS A CAMERA IN THE CLASSROOM ALL DAY, SENDING PICTURES TO THE INTERNET, SO THAT PARENTS CAN SEE WHAT THEIR CHILDREN ARE UP TO?

SIMPLICITY ITSELF. JUST ONE MORE BENEFIT FROM MY VAST REPERTOIRE!

CAMERAS? PARENTS? UP TO?

YES, IT'S SUPPOSE TO BE SO THAT THE PARENTS CAN MAKE SURE THEIR CHILDREN ARE HAPPY, BUT IN YOUR CASE SCROGGINS...

IN MY CASE... ME MUM WOULD SEE ME PICKING ME NOSE INSTEAD OF WORKING? ME DAD WOULD SPOT ME FIRING INK-BALLS AT SARAH HEATHCOTE? THEY'D SEE ME PULLING RUDE FACES BEHIND YOUR BACK?

146

Crashing fact

In practice, a good combination is that of a human teacher using computers as a tool to help make their teaching better – or, in some cases, possible at all. Where it's not possible for a student to get to college, for instance, computer links and electronic mail can make all the difference.

At the end of a course, a professor received a message from a student saying: "One of the things I really appreciate about the course is that none of you realized that I was disabled."

To which the professor, who used a speaking computer, replied: "And you didn't know I was blind."

Coming Soon-To A Computer Near You

One thing's for sure. If computers are playing a big part in today's world, they'll be playing an even bigger part in tomorrow's. But how big? Well, for a start, we could be seeing headlines like this...

Computer drives pupil round the bend!

▶ Instead of slapping on the L-plates, jumping into a car and then heading out on to the road to terrify real people, you could be made to learn on a computer first. A car-driving VR system will put you behind the wheel of a virtual car – and test you! You won't be allowed into a real car until you pass.

VROOM!
VROOM!

IT HAS ITS OWN SOUND EFFECTS, THANK YOU

▶ Once out on the road, you'll be driving a car that won't let you break the speed limit. An in-car computer system will read information from road signs and prevent your car going any faster, however hard you press the accelerator!

A SNAIL CARRYING HEAVY SHOPPING COULD GO FASTER THAN THIS!

ONLY IF IT HAD A DRIVING LICENCE

▶ There'll still be road works and traffic jams, of course. But another computer will help you avoid them. Programmed with your destination, it will send you personal traffic information to warn you about hold-ups ahead. It will even tell you a better way to go.

▶ That still won't guarantee you'll get to your destination quickly, though. Not only will traffic lights still be around, they'll be clever traffic lights! For a start they'll be able to recognize a police car or ambulance when it's coming and change to let it through.

NEE-NAW!
NEE-NAW!

YOU CAN'T CHEAT

▶ Worse (or better) than that, traffic lights will be capable of pollution busting. By sensing that pollution is building up, whole groups of lights will be able to change their way of working so as to keep some vehicles on the move at the expense of others. You could be stuck on a red light for hours!

Crashing fact

Will it be worth learning to drive at all? Maybe it will be better just to stay at home and play a VR car racing game. Based on real race tracks, these games are already fantastically good – so good that world champion Jacques Villeneuve used one to learn all the bends and turns before he got to the real track! What you might call a stop-me-crashing computer game!

I don't feel well!

Another area in which computers are playing an ever greater part is medicine. Try this quick quiz to discover just how "big" a part...

1 You wake up with a terrible pain in your toe. In fact it's so bad you can't get up. How do you get to see the doctor?

   a You hop to the surgery.
   b The doctor visits you.
   c Both you and the doctor stay put.

Answer: c. A one-to-one video-computer link will let the doctor examine you without either of you moving. (This already happens in the USA for groups of bed-ridden patients.)

2 It's bad news. You need an operation on your toe. How will the surgeon work out where to stick the scalpel?

   a By doing the operation.
   b By drawing a diagram.
   c By taking an X-ray.

Answer: a, with a bit of c. Doctors will feed the X-ray images into a computer and build up a 3-dimensional model of your body. They'll then test out the operation by performing it on the computer before trying it on you!

3 It's the day of the operation. Who wields the scalpel?

   a The surgeon.

b A robot.
c You.

Answer: b, controlled by a. It will be possible for operations to be carried out by a robot, with the human surgeon controlling its movements over a video link!

4 Disaster! A week after your operation, your toe becomes infected. Back you go to hospital – where you're visited by a robot! What has it been specially designed to do?

   a Bite.
   b Sniff.
   c Kiss.

Answer: b. And not because biting is for toma-toes and kissing happens under the miste-toe! Different bacteria give off different smells. A robot with an electronic "nose" will be able to compare the pong from your bad toe against a list of known whiffs and work out what the infection is. That way, exactly the right medicine can be prescribed for your toe at once. (In other words, you won't have to wait until toe-morrow). What's more, the robot will always ready for action – because it can't catch a cold!

THIS IS OUR LATEST SNIFFING ROBOT

Crashing fact

If you're an asthma sufferer then computer technology will soon be helping you, too. When the doctor listens to your breathing, he or she will be using a "smart" stethoscope which will display information on how your lungs are working. Then, when you're given an inhaler to use, that will have a chip in it as well so that you get just the right amount of inhalant at any time.

You will meet a tall, dark, handsome computer...

Computers are so much a part of life nowadays that it's easy to forget how fast they've developed. If your parents and grandparents look as blank as a turned-off screen when you show them your computer, don't think it's because they're dumb. When they were your age, things were very different:

Then again, when they left school, it wasn't so hard to find a job because:

BEFORE COMPUTERS, BUSINESSES USED MORE PEOPLE TO ADD UP NUMBERS...

I'VE RUN OUT OF FINGERS AGAIN!

CASHIER

I'D LIKE £20 OF PENNIES, PLEASE

BEFORE CASH MACHINES BANKS USED MORE CLERKS TO GIVE OUT MONEY...

TIGHTEN THESE BOLTS BEFORE LUNCH!

BEFORE ROBOTS, MANUFACTURERS USED MORE WORKERS TO BUILD THINGS...

So, computers can be good for you – and they can be bad for you! How will things change over the next fifty years? If you could time-travel forward, what would you find?

Here are some predictions of what computers will be doing in the year 2050. Will their new abilities be good – or bad? You decide!

High-tech houses

Everything in a house will be computer-controlled: the lights, the heating, the video-doorbell, the garage doors, the bath taps – everything. What's more, the computer will accept spoken commands, and be able to reply.

Good fun, and very convenient. **Bad** news if the computer thinks you've said "turn on the tap" when you actually said, "let out the cat". **Very bad** news if your parents have set the computer to ask where you're going and what time you'll be back ... and to lock the doors if you don't reply!

What a load of rubbish!

Even rubbish bins will be computerised. They'll read the bar codes on thrown-away food packages and send a message to the home computer which will add the item to your souped-up supermarket loyalty card. When you arrive at the supermarket you'll have your card read at the *check-in*. Then, as you go round, the store computer will send messages to a speaker in your trolley telling you what you need to buy.

Good for those who hate writing shopping lists or have bad memories. **Bad** for those who can't resist a supermarket computer whispering, "Go on, be a devil. Forget your diet and treat yourself. You know you haven't had a giant box of those fantastically expensive chocolates for ages…"

School's out – for ever!

You'll learn your lessons at home instead. You'll have a video-connection to your teachers so that you can see them, and they can see you.

Good because it means you can be taught by the best teachers, even if you live hundreds of miles away from them. **Bad** if it means you can't do all the other things you do at school like making new friends, having a laugh, playing about … and meeting real live teachers. Who will you be able to poke fun at?

Great games

Computer games will be totally realistic. You'll play them in a portable games booth with a wrap-around screen that puts you into the game. You'll also wear a cybersuit – a special suit which passes information to the computer about every movement you make. That way you won't just press keys and have your heroes fight the villain for you – you'll actually wave your arms and kick your legs and do the fighting yourself!

Good for games players, because it will give amazing realism – but **bad** if it means having night-mares afterwards. (Not to mention the **bad** news of suddenly wanting to go to the loo when you're strapped into your cybersuit – or finding the jungle exploration game you're playing has gone wrong and is telling the suit to give you the experience of being crushed by a boa constrictor!)

Been there, done that!

Virtual Reality will be extended to cover all sorts of experiences. You'll be able to go on holiday to a VR Bahamas, wander through a VR pyramid, climb a VR Mount Everest and swim in a VR Pacific Ocean. You'll be able to spend more time in virtual worlds than the real world!

Good if it enables people to enjoy experiences they'd never be able to have in any other way. **Bad** if – like TV addicts who think soap characters are real – they start having trouble dealing with real life.

Thumbs up!

If you open a bank account, your fingerprints will be stored on the bank's computer. Thereafter, whenever you want to take money out of a cash machine you'll have to prove your identity by putting your finger or thumb into a special reader.

Good for banks, and their customers, because it will prevent criminals using stolen bank cards to steal money. **Bad** if your fingerprints don't only stay on the bank's computer but find their way onto a police computer even though you've not done anything wrong!

> I COULDN'T HAVE ROBBED THE BANK LAST NIGHT, I WAS WATCHING TELLY-TUBBIES!

> WE'VE GOT YOUR FINGER-PRINTS, KID!

So, will these predictions come true? Who knows. Even the experts have got it wrong in the past...

Charles Duell, Commissioner of the US Patent Office, in 1899

Thomas Watson, chairman of IBM, in 1943

Kenneth Olsen, President of Digital Equipment Corporation, in 1977

One thing is for sure, though. Computers are here to stay. Which means that there'll be plenty of them working in the years to come – and plenty of them that will do just the opposite!
So here's one final prediction:

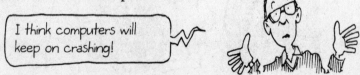

Michael Coleman in 1999